Lilac Time at the Rodeo: Stories of Identity, AIDS & Fashion

For Roma,

Mark Joseph Russell

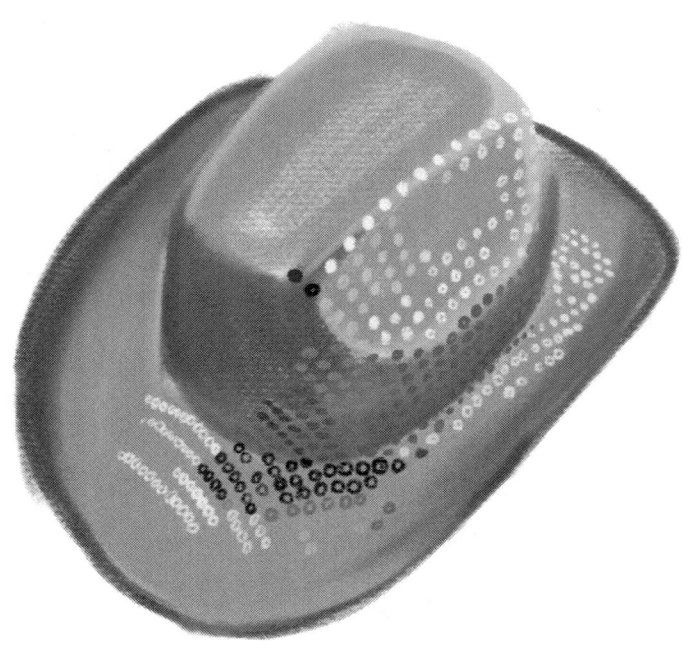

Figure 1 "Sequin Stetson" @Mark O'Connell 2021

ISBN: 9798546958596

Imprint: Independently published
Follow me on socials!

Instagram

@MARKOCONNELLSTUDIO

TikTok: @markoconnell176

markoconnellstudio

♪ TikTok

LinkedIn:

Dr. Mark Joseph O'Connell
Professor at Seneca Polytechnic

Facebook: markoconnellstudio

X: ProfMOConnell

Illustrations

Table of Contents

Footfall

Sprawling relaxed, asleep,
On his ebony bed adorned with coral eagles,
Comfortable in the vigour of his flesh,
The prime of his youth,
Callous, unheeding, imperial,
On sleeps Nero.

But out in the marble hallway
The lares, the little household gods
Of his ancestors, the Aenobarbi,
Stand shuffling in their shrine,
Uneasy, trembling.
They have heard that dreaded sound
The din of doom ascending,
The tramp of iron shaking the stairs.
Then one moves, and the next,
Scurrying to the back of their shrine
Pushing and tripping, falling over each other,
All the lares, the tiny gods,
Trying to hide as best they can.
They have learned the footfall of the Furies.

Constantine Cavafy, "Footfall" 1909, *Poetry* 1947, (132)

Preface: Not the First Rodeo

1983, Reno, Nevada, anonymous phone calls to all three of the main television stations warned of potential sniper fire. There was however a bigger threat to the Gay Rodeo that year. It was of course: AIDS. Another concealed, lethal, menace that was stripping the Gay community of all the hard-won gains of the previous twenty years...

Rodeo, the idea of performing on a bucking bronco in a ring, with spectators watching. Rodeo, the expression "this ain't my first rodeo", been through this. Also, the idea of Rodeo Drive which is pronounced in the Spanish way: Rodayo; and therefore, has a chic connotation. That insider knowledge, the je ne sais quoi, is *so* very Gay. (The antithesis is of course the scene in *Showgirls* where Nomi pronounces Versace not with a "chi", but with an "ace".)

Then there is the Reno Gay Rodeo. Set up by Phil Ragsdale who "wanted to create a space for the LGBTQ+ community to express themselves openly"; and as a way for "...supposedly straight rodeo people (to) do something with other people that were like them" in order that "They could actually be themselves". The previous year had been the apex of the event "With around 20,000 people at the event, led by Joan Rivers [who else!], the grand marshal" (Zender 2019). Then AIDS hit and decimated the event even as it was simultaneously decimating the lives and social fabric of Gay culture everywhere.

9

It was impossible, it was *horrific*, it happened.

Unfortunately, the "gay rodeo in Reno disappeared" (Zender 2019). For a while it looked like Gay culture in general would disappear along with that rodeo. Thankfully it didn't, but the damage from the fallout of AIDS was still catastrophic.

Our Gay cowboys dismounted and wandered bowlegged out into a hazy desert horizon; they were beckoned and welcomed into an eternal lilac twilight by all who had come before...

Figure 2 "Cowboys at the Barn" @Mark O'Connell 2021

Introduction: The Innocents

"The first Nazi book burning, I would have you remember, was of a gay and lesbian archive." (660)

Paul Monette, *The Politics of Silence,*1993.

I have been seeing a lot of Dr. Anthony Fauci recently, all over the media talking about the Covid-19 pandemic that is threatening the global population, it has brought back a lot of memories. *Bad* memories from a different time, and a visceral re-engagement with an earlier pandemic: AIDS. Truly, déjà vu of the worst sort. The fevered discussions around how to protect oneself, the shifting understandings regarding transmission, the barrage of contradictory messaging, the conspiracy theories, (the lies!), the fevered paranoic whispers of a disease that was manufactured in a government lab, it is all so familiar to me *now* because it all was part of public discourse *then*.

Memory…to this day there are times I think "Oh, he would love this…" and then remember my "he" has been dead for thirty years now. I write this for "him", partially to remember, and partially as a love letter to lost friends and lovers. The subjects of this book (and the subsequent *Rodeo* books) are Queer fashion and art practitioners. These people because of the stigma attached to their illness, were never properly eulogized: Chester

Weinberg, Halston, and Way Bandy. Bright, brilliant, and visionary all, the loss of these men to AIDS was devastating.

In some cases, the memory of the oeuvres of my subjects is fading, in others prurient focus on the details of their lives overshadow the work, in others they are now forgotten or excised from art and fashion history entirely. This is not only an injustice to their legacies it leaves a disrupted chronology of Queer history.

It also leaves some really wild and wonderful stories, as yet, untold. The idea in my writings is to not only to focus on their premature AIDS related mortalities, but also to remember the vibrant and beautiful work that they produced, and how they *lived*. And by so doing, draw attention to the fact that their creative trajectories, their budding careers were cut horrifically short.

We lost so much potential during those years, and while there were some like Keith Haring and Derek Jarman who were catalyzed by their diagnosis, driven by the desperate potentiality of their imminent demise to create superlative work, yet they *all* ultimately left their symphonies unfinished. It is this "lost generation" of men I would like to shine a light on.

The main reason I am writing this though, is because I kept waiting for someone *else* to publish about this subject, I desperately wanted to read it. Unfortunately, there is a definite lack of socio-critical work published on the eighties and early 90's AIDS era in fashion; and I honestly believe it is because the people who could write it are either dead or too traumatized by that time period.

(The latter was true for me for a very long time.) Valerie Steele, fashion historian, theorist and director of the Museum at FIT is the only one I know of who has published in-depth valuable research on this subject in the fashion academic arena.

As I detail later, even my engagement with AIDS-related literature was sporadic (pathetic), entirely due to burying my own head in the sand; equal parts cowardice, and self-preservation. Not only was I not writing it, I could not even bear to read about it.

As per Edmund White, AIDS is not a topic that people want to read about:

> ...[I]t's like trying to get a child to swallow cod liver oil. Nobody wants to read about AIDS. People who have it don't want to read about it because it's depressing. People who don't have it but are susceptible to HIV don't want to read about it because it's bad news. The only thing people want to read about AIDS is the headline that says they found a cure. you can walk into bookstores and see piles of AIDS book remainders: nobody wants to read them. (125)

Nobody wants to read them! I did not want to read about AIDS, not only did I not read about it I did not even want to *think* about it if I could help it.

For this reason (among others: apathy, trauma, trepidation), I kept waiting for someone better qualified, smarter, more eloquent, to write about this monumental loss, to properly eulogize, to remember, to bear witness. And then there was Covid and I was faced with so much of what happened the first time around, ignorance, misinformation, paranoia. It was taking over my thoughts, entering in through my dreams.

I write of the talented and (in)famous (and for the most part Gay and male) but that in no way detracts from the stories of anyone else lost to AIDS. I do not write in depth about the women we have lost to AIDS in this monograph, and there are so many of them as well, Gia Carangi the lesbian supermodel who was only 26 when she died, Cookie Mueller, Alexis Arquette who were also (in)famous; millions were not. Elizabeth, the wife of actor Paul Michael Glaser of Starsky & Hutch fame who caught AIDS from a transfusion while giving birth, and unknowingly passed the virus to her infant daughter Ariel (1981-1988) via breastfeeding. Also, the lovely Ali Gertz a young woman from Park Avenue privilege who contracted HIV from a one-night stand with a Studio 54 bartender when she was sixteen. Then there are Burt Reynolds and Isabelle Adjani, only two of many celebrities falsely rumored to be living with HIV at one time or another either because of unexpected rapid weight loss or association with friends who were living with AIDS. It was reliable tabloid fodder.

Figure 4 "Burt Reynolds" @Mark O'Connell 2021

Children were also caught up in the hysteria and horror of the first years of the pandemic. The truly devastating experiences of Ricky, Robert, and Randy Ray, then 10, 9 & 8 respectively, three boys with hemophilia whose family home in Florida was firebombed one August night in 1987 (Cox, 2007). The family lost everything and had to leave town. Their crime? They had been actively trying to enrol their boys in school when this act of localized terrorism occurred.

There were also straight men who contracted AIDS. Jamaica Kincaid describes in her poignant but devastating memoir of her brother's death in Antigua in her memoir *My Brother* (1997). He is arguably one who is not spoken of when discussing AIDS: a young Rastafarian male, presumably straight. Kincaid does not know how her brother contracted HIV, she does not believe it was from IV drug use and has no reason to believe him to be involved in homosexual activities. Nevertheless, he is dying when she receives the word and gets on a plane with a prescription for the very expensive drug AZT. She notes that it is the only AZT on the entire island of Antigua at that time. She visits him in the hospital and the memories reawaken:

> He was not born in this hospital. Of my mother's four children, he was the one born at home. I remember him being born. I was thirteen years of age then. We had just finished eating our supper, a supper of boiled fish and bread and butter, and my mother sent me to fetch the midwife, a woman named Nurse Stevens... (Kincaid 1997, 6)

Kincaid was much older and took care of her brother as an infant, but as he was only three when she left Antigua, they did not have a close relationship. One of the shocks that the news of his illness brought to her was that she realized he loved him.

And then there was Ryan White, eventually becoming the most famous (non-Gay) diagnosed with AIDS in the early years of the plague. In his early teens, he wanted to

16

go to school and faced unrelenting hostility and obstacles. His story caught the attention of the news agencies as well as Elton John and Michael Jackson. The latter eventually wrote the song "Gone to Soon" to eulogize his young friend. White was one of those living with HIV who was categorized as an "innocent victim", in contrast to the "guilty" Gay men, sex workers and IV drug users who were cast as receiving the just retribution for their "sinful transgressions". There was a common media portrayal of them, due to their "innocence", they had been the victims of *undeserved* hostility and hatred. Their stories were used as ways to humanize the AIDS crisis. To reclaim the narrative from Gay men and IV drug users. This was a widely communicated narrative of the plague years but was one contested, notably even by White himself before he died (Bryan-Wilson 2021 [2017], 196). Also, the reality of African AIDS awareness is that it was always a heterosexual population that was affected by it, and they were denied care due to poverty, and lack of access to medications that were developed in more affluent countries.

I do not write about these people because their loss is any less tragic, or their lives of less importance. Also, not because a writer should be prohibited, should not write about those who are different from them (they should, respectfully though). No, it is because as Simon Doonan states in *The Asylum: A Collage of Couture Reminiscences... and Hysteria* (2013): "I cannot list everyone. This book would turn into War and Peace" (131). Indeed. Still, they are all people who died, wonderful people, each and every one of them an individual. These stories are heartbreaking. The North American experience was also one mitigated by

---

inequitable medical resources made available to those living HIV because it was framed as this "Gay" plague. The ignorance of those around them, the hatred. That fear. They all suffered terribly, and unnecessarily. No one deserved or deserves to die from AIDS. They are all *gone too soon*!

The New Orleans Jazz Funeral Procession

"'At first America had trouble with people with AIDS,?' The announcer says in that falsely conversational tone, that tended to be reassuring about apocalyptic things. 'But then, they came around.'

I almost crash the car.

Oh no, I think. *Now this.* Now after all this death and all this pain and all this unbearable truth about persecution, suffering, and the indifference of the protected, *Now* they're going to pretend that *naturally*, *normally* things just happened to get better." (2)

Sarah Schulman, *The Gentrification of the Mind*, 2012.

Revisionist history is also emerging as something that needs to be considered as well: "...it's hard to have collective memory when so many who were 'there' are not 'here'" (Schulman 2012, 135). Setting the record straight so to speak. Although my ambitions are certainly polemic for this book. (Spoiler alert: I was there during the worst of the worst of the AIDS years, I hated what I saw and how people were treated, and I *am* an older angry Queer now.) I would therefore like to take some time to eulogize the "guilty", who also were subjected to unspeakable hostilities and cruelties even as they fought for their lives. It is this "lost generation" of men I would like to shine a light on. Ultimately, while there is certainly an elegiac tone to be found in some of this book, it is also meant to function as something of a fabulous soirée, to be celebratory of those bright spirits who are no longer with us. It would be a disservice to my subjects if my book was not also as lively and colourful as they themselves often were. An effervescent New Orleans Jazz funeral procession then, as opposed to a stultifying somber wake. These men were brilliant and FABULOUS, and they would demand no less for any narrative chronicling their creative oeuvres.

Reflections on a Happy Birthday

Like Simon Doonan, visual merchandiser extraordinaire, I am *d'un certain age*. I was at a fiftieth birthday party (mine), and I was speaking to a friend about the early '90s. I was describing some of the research I was doing, and my memories from that time. He opened up about a former lover who was one of the earliest to develop full-blown AIDS in Canada: also, a man whose family for whatever reason, religious or otherwise, would have nothing to do with him. So, my friend rallied a group to bring food into the hospital to take care of him, to bathe him, to look after him, because the hospital staff were not willing to do so. The dying man was isolated, alone in a room. He died. The friends reached out to the family who for two days refused to even pick up the body. My friend just asked that he be involved in the funeral arrangements and know what was going to happen. They never heard from the family again…they do not know where their friend is buried.

This is not an uncommon story for the survivors of the late 1980s and early '90s. Before medicine caught up with lives that were being ripped apart, and abruptly ended. People didn't know what was going on with the illness and they were terrified.

I put my arm around my friend who by the end of recounting his story was starting to feel those old emotions and was visibly upset. I said to him "that wasn't normal", none of that was normal, to have young men dying all around. It was like a war. Slowly he said "it was not normal" as he choked back tears.

Chapter One: "Chester Weinberg, Fire on the Island and The Boy from Brooklyn"

Figure 8 "Chester Weinberg" @Mark O'Connell 2021

Slow Down You Move too Fast

"'Never love a wild thing, Mr. Bell,' Holly advised him. 'That was Doc's mistake. He was always lugging home wild things. A hawk with a hurt wing. One time it was a full-grown bobcat with a broken leg. But you can't give your heart to a wild thing: the more you do, the stronger they get. Until they're strong enough to run into the woods. Or fly into a tree. Then a taller tree. Then the sky. That's how you'll end up, Mr. Bell. If you let yourself love a wild thing. You'll end up looking at the sky."

— Truman Capote, Breakfast at Tiffany's (1958)

I recently purchased a second-hand book, and let me tell you, it is one satisfying publication. One of those specifically 70s-era genre coffee table type books, with many gorgeous photographs (all black & white) with a depth and richness that comes from shooting with film. Inspired by new journalistic directions of the era, there is a Time magazine layout quality to the oversized photographs that support the text. Graphics, text and photos all work together. Breaking down boundaries. a cinéma vérité quality has been imparted to all of them. The subjects are designers, at work, in their homes, the Laurens are at the beach with Ralph's Porsche in the sand, Edith Head is photographed standing at the top of a flight of stairs, small and immaculate in her crisp white skirt suit and those dark rimmed glasses, at the threshold of her workroom that produced gowns for the most glamorous of Hollywood's sirens. Lilly Daché leans back in repose on a chair upholstered with an oversized organic graphic, strands of shell necklaces around her neck, her elbow brushing up against a Picasso ceramic urn that holds the cutting from a particularly exotic breed of orchid. Oscar de la Renta pokes his head out from beneath a huge palm leaf, beaming. Charles James, in a shiny black leather jacket, leans up against the sign of his residence: the Chelsea Hotel. Elsa Perretti turns partially away from the viewer, pensively looks back and up, her backdrop is Gaudi's la Sagrada Família cathedral in Barcelona. Bill Blass, perched on a ledge tosses an apple, the shutter snaps at the exact moment the apple obscures his eyes and nose, a Magritte composition; off in the distance the Queensborough bridge—immortalized in Simon & Garfunkel's "The 59th St. Bridge Song (Feeling Groovy)"—spans the East River and stretches off into Long Island City.

This book [my treasured second-hand bookstore find] is called *The Fashion Makers* (1974), and it is the collaborative effort of Barbra Walz who is the photographer, and instigated the project, and Bernadine Morris legendary NYT fashion critic who is credited with the text. (Kevin Walz, the photographer's husband is the graphic designer of the book.) The very 70s artful relaxed pose is as much a subject as the profiles of the forty-nine designers profiled.

You know they were working it, but it still comes across as unforced, playful even. Their respective environs were presented as something casual, but make no mistake, they were beautifully and *artfully* presented.

———

23

This "fun" was very well designed. As was much of the naturalism of the 70's era of peak modernism.

There is a photograph within that publication that I have studied closely, it is on a two-page spread. Also, black-and-white, it shows two men, they have wonderful grins on their faces. They stand on a raised boardwalk; the ocean spreads out behind them as they are situated on the crest of a tall dune. It has to be Fire Island, I'm sure I've actually been on that boardwalk before. It is situated in The Pines:

> The Pines is a mile long grid of boardwalks connecting about 600 homes built on telephone pole stilts sunk into a sandbar. The island is a thirty-six mile long barrier a few miles off the Long Island coast protecting it from Atlantic storms. A thirty-minute ferry ride from Sayville crosses the great South Bay into the harbor. Back then you could also take off from Manhattan's East River and land in the bay. (Bianchi 2013, 7)

The Pines, a train and ferry ride from Manhattan, a mythical locus of Queer desire and freedom. And traditionally a reliable (if vulnerable) refuge from judgment, persecution and societal homophobia:

> The Pines affords a psychic distance from the noise of the city in a natural landscape all the more beautiful for its fragility. The houses float above a shape shifting sand bar, precious, as beauty is, for its vulnerability. Hurricanes blow through, wash away homes and pools here and there, and reset the beach. But the pines endures. Flexible in the face of traumatic force. (Bianchi 2013, 7)

The history of the Pines is one of a "people who had felt like outcasts finding community" (Rawlins qtd. in Trebay 2013). They congregated, communed, and erected their promised land on the beach. It was there that Truman Capote wrote "Breakfast at Tiffany's" in the 1950's (Verga 2019). Marilyn Monroe, Elizabeth Taylor, and a lot of A-lister Gay men [including Montgomery Clift *sigh] all hung out there, but like everyone else, they walked to their summer stays along the raised boardwalks.

Although an overwhelmingly male milieu, it does not feel restrictive. Gay men have children after all, and they have parents, siblings, and straight friends all of whom could be found in and around The Pines. Although *way* too expensive, it had an equalizing effect nonetheless; you knew right away that you are not in East Hampton.

It is also the only beach paradise I know of that you can easily access by public transit: subway, a train, a ferry, ten-minute walk across the island and I am standing with my feet in the churning surf gratefully breathing in that humid, salty ocean air.

Where many oceanside summer spots have a pleasant disorder and lack of pretension—you and your family descend from the beach house perched high up on stilts, walk across the highway in bare feet to the Dairy Queen and have your nightly ice cream, or drive up the road a bit for lobster at a splintery picnic table. Not The Pines, which has a consistency of architecture, and a very particular visual vernacular. Beach houses there are a living example of a "sustainable modernism in cedar and glass that was as attuned to natural landscapes as to our animal natures" (Rawlins & Gordon 2013). Monumental and monolithic are not normally terms applied to beach houses, but you just need to gaze upon these beauties, to see how well the descriptors fit. The beach houses of The Pines are built around a careful geometry, they possess a spare angularity, but the ubiquitous hard-edged minimalist aesthetic is softened by the tempered cedar of their construction, their exteriors have been greyed by the weather to matte silver and pewter; also blackish hues inflected with a bitter cocoa. They are a Cubist fantasy come to life, all tight angles and grayscale. These elegant edifices are all reflected in their accompanying pools, as if Louis Kahn's severe but sculptural aesthetic for the *Jatiyo Sangsad Bhaban*, the National Assembly Building of Bangladesh, situated in Dhaka was expanded and applied to an entire Atlantic oceanic village.

The town is criss crossed by raised walkways which serve as "streets". These freaked me out a little at first, as I am one of those tall men who bump into things. I walk into doorframes, I often stub my toes, always slightly off balance (I get this from my father whose expletives could often be heard echoing throughout my parent's townhouse as he impacted some immovable object or other). Clumsy at the best of times I marvel that heavily inebriated men navigate this community without tumbling over the edge and breaking limbs. (Tom Bianchi recounts witnessing Steve Rubell of Studio 54 fame actually taking a plunge over the edge once.) Surrounding the architecture, and the raised boardwalks though is much overgrown lush nature, the fecundity of the living environment is in no way restricted; it thus "naturalizes" what could have been stark and arid, instead shrubs, bushes, vines, grasses, and trees, can be observed to overhang, entwine, and generally insinuate themselves into the built environment everywhere you turn. The

Pines is actually one of the most beautiful places I have ever visited. It is truly a floating world on a sandbar.

The building of this enclave was not happenstance. A certain logic and ethos has shaped the principles of design and engagement found here. Within these super modern beach houses, contained by all that chic cedar that has been abraded and grayed out by the elements, are tall arching great common rooms, surrounded by small bedrooms, all looking out onto their serene pool decks, the surrounding abundant verdancy, and then to the ocean beyond.

Horace Gifford was one of the key architects (literally) of this community. Gifford a native Floridian who actually studied under Louis Kahn at the University of Pennsylvania in the 1950's designed forty homes in The Pines and was highly influential in shaping the unique architectural aesthetic that is found here. His style for the built environment evolved as a symbiotic reflection of the evolution of the growth of gay consciousness and autonomy: "Gifford's serene 1960s pavilions provided refuge from a hostile world, while his exuberant post-Stonewall, pre-AIDS masterpieces orchestrated bacchanals of liberation" (Gifford 2013). They were designed for communal living, and *definitely* for display:

> [E]legant, stark structures [built] on this austerely beautiful and fragile barrier island, houses of naturally weathering cedar, redwood pavilions set back from the boardwalk, their broad windows serving as prosceniums across which backlighted players in Speedos, or else nothing, played out a specific variant of the theater of late 20th century gay life. (Trebay 2013, pgh. 3)

Yes, they were also designed for a lot of free spirited communal lovin'! What happened in those gorgeous beach houses, within the Meat Rack (a park that separates The Pines from his more boho neighbour: the sapphic-inflected and delicious Cherry Grove) as well as in the surf on the beach sometimes is the stuff of hedonistic Queer legend, and "was probably a natural outgrowth of what happens when you repress a people for 2,500 years" (Trebay 2013) Yee-haw! An elegant visual vernacular, that juxtaposes with a throbbing sexual intensity, now that is *so* Gay.

A Photo

The two men pictured in the photograph are Calvin Klein and Chester Weinberg. Klein is much taller than Weinberg and stands behind him, his arm casually draped over his friend's shoulder, as he playfully rubs his head. It is not a sexy or innuendo-inflected photo by any means. It looks like Klein is ready to give Chester a bare-knuckle-to-pate noogie. The body language is very relaxed, they could be brothers, they could be lovers, they could be Gay they could just as easily be straight, they certainly seem to be best buddies. It doesn't matter really as the ideal word to describe the vibe in this photo is "camaraderie". They are both laughing and obviously having fun in this photograph.

Now you ask me, "I know Calvin, but who is Chester?"

Chester Weinberg died on the 24th of April 1985, in New York City. Like you most likely, I had not heard of him before, not until I saw an internet posting briefly describing his life and work. Intrigued, I did a little more digging and came across the article "The Day AIDS Hit the Fashion Industry: Thirty Years Ago, Seventh Avenue Lost its First Designer to the Disease During a Time When People Were Afraid to Even Say its Name" (2015) in *The Atlantic*. Authored by Kimberly Chrisman-Campbell, her research made it clear that Weinberg was someone I definitely needed to know more about. Further investigation led me to track down and purchase *The Fashion Makers*, which I have in turn both used to breathe life into as well as ground this chapter.

So, let me tell you a little bit about Chester!

He was a lifelong New Yorker, and his career was entirely dedicated to fashion. As recounted by Morris in her excellent *Fashion Makers* text, Chester Weinberg was a "poor boy from Brooklyn who knew nothing of the world of fashion until he started high school. Described as "a small, wispy boy" Weinberg attended the High School of Music and Art when he was not yet even in his teens. (Walz & Morris 1978, 219). Dubbed the "castle on the hill" up in Harlem, other notable alumni are: Al Jaffee; Bess Myerson; Billy Dee Williams; Milton Glaser; Eartha Kitt; Hal Linden; Shari Lewis (nee Sonia Phyllis Hurwitz); Diahann Carroll; Erica Jong; Steven Bochco; Laura Nyro; Maira Kalman, Melissa Manchester; Isaac Mizrahi and Slick Rick. (From the graduating classes of: 1940; 1941; 1955; 1947; 1948; 1948; c. 1951;1953; 1959; 1961; 1965; 1967; 1968; 1979 and 1983 respectively.) (LaGuardia notable alumni)

...Melissa Manchester!!!, also Milton Glaser...*hello.* Weinberg is not listed as a "notable" alumnus on the website of The Laguardia school which was a later evolution of his alma mater. This plainly speaks to his erasure from fashion history.

Of his time at High School of Music and Art, Weinberg recalled: "That's when I saw my first Claire McCardell dress..." and many other historical fashion objects, and for him, that introduction to fashion was "mind blowing". He recounted the subsequent redirection of his interests:

> [I]t was art I was interested in then. When I had this exposure, I realized for the first time that instead of being the head of the art department in a local high school, I could become a fashion designer. (Weinberg qtd. in Morris & Walz 1974, 219)

He then went on to study fashion at Parson's.

Figure 9 Claire McCardell Illustration" @Mark O'Connell 2021

Barely sixteen when he started college he was remembered as a "brilliant student". Years later, he was still referred to as "my baby", by Ann Keagy, who was one of his professors and later ran the illustrious fashion department (219). He graduated in 1951, first in his class.

Then it was time for the "apprenticeship". He entered the fashion industry during the 1950's 7th Avenue rag trade era. American industry was gearing up to supply the post-war prosperity of 50's America. It was high volume, high pressure [when is it not though? Fashion is no place for the faint of heart]. Weinberg slogged away in "Seventh Avenue's back rooms, striving always to get into higher priced houses so he could work with better fabrics, try more inventive designs". He recalled some highlights of this era: "I went to Europe, I saw Balenciaga, I was invited to Jack Fath's parties, danced with Ginger Rogers at Schiaparelli." There were also challenges: "I was discouraged because American designers, including me were copying Europe. I wanted the American thing to begin to happen." (219-220). American design was not yet valued, that would soon change.

Figure 10 "Chester Weinberg Gown" @Mark O'Connell 2021

The 1960's was a time when American designers were indeed "coming of age", more and more they were released from the back rooms and brought out front and centre to put a face to the brand. They were also "invited to fashionable dinner parties. They decorated charity balls. [and] Society women came to their openings." (Weinberg qtd. in Morris & Walz 1974, 219). Weinberg identified with Geoffrey Beene as a designer who was making a reputation for himself and supporting the fledgling ontology of a uniquely American style: "I followed his career with admiration", he recalls. "I identified with him. When I heard he was leaving to start his own firm, I wondered who would get his job", he recalled that "It was a plumb job". When Geoffrey Beene was given star billing at Teal Traina, Weinberg felt the shift was starting to happen. It was Weinberg who was tapped to follow Beene at Teal Traina, but his name would not be added to the label as Beene's had been prominently featured previously. Already, "Manufacturers were...leery of giving a designer too much exposure for fear they would do exactly what Geoffrey Beene did: start his own business." Three years later Weinberg jumped ship. 1966 saw the debut of an eponymous collection with "Chester Weinberg on the door and on the label." (220). WWD profiled the new venture on Monday November 7th, 1966, in "The Fashions: New York Advance: Chester Weinberg". Weinberg's spring collection for 1967 was shown in a double page spread of the daily fashion newspaper wherein they noted his "Camellia theme" and described a "whole series of nifty navy dresses with crisp white touches. here is his belted look in two ways - one high, one bloused- both in navy wool crepe" (WWD 1966 pgh 1). The spread was accompanied by a [quite gorgeous] gestural fashion illustration in charcoal, showing these new looks in motion on a figure. "Watch for Chester's short sleeves set in very high" (WWD 1966 pgh 1) they extolled. As a result of this collection, he was:

> [C]atapulted into the rarefied circle of big names in American fashion. It was an exceptional kind of collection. At a time when tough chic was in, he made pretty dresses. Instead of hard edged tailoring, he used ruffles. Suit jackets were shapely. For evening, there were long organdy dresses. "It was really opposing Courrèges," [Weinberg] said. "I didn't think clothes should be so severe. I thought women ought to look pretty" (Walz & Morris 1978, 220).

He capitalized on his initial success and further innovated: "Turning to matte jersey. He pared down his designs, always simplifying". He simplified, but not without playful touches, as "He put a peace button on his bridal dress." It was smooth sailing until the 1970 "debacle of the midi" which was to prove the downfall of his eponymous line (Walz & Morris 1978, 220). The notorious midi was a 1970 fashion offering that sought to render the entire miniskirt trend of the 1960's obsolete, passé. It was a mid-calf grazing style, that harkened back to the 1940's. It turns out, women liked their short skirts thank you very much, and they were not about to cover up those legs again. The "stylish wife of a Chicago lawyer" was quoted on the front page of the WSJ stating that "midis repelled her", and that she felt that "in this day of dissent and liberation, it amazes me that the fashion industry can be so coercive". The client in this case proved to be remarkably recalcitrant and was not to be coerced: "Ker-plunk...that's right, fashion fans, that's the sound of the star herself, entering the marketplace, tripping on her own hemline and falling flat on her face…" (WSJ 1970, 1) .The midi was a significant moment in fashion, it was the first time that fashion buyers rejected outright a style that was rolled out en masse, and had this affect their purchases (or lack thereof) of unrelated styles. Disaster. The "moribund midi" was called "sleazy, dowdy and depressing" and in this case: "the lower the hem, the lower the sales" (WSJ 1970, 1). This particular look just ran counter to the zeitgeist and was an obvious ploy to arbitrarily change up the silhouette. It blew up in the face of retailers who were then stuck with a volume of unsold goods, as well as a very angry customer base.

This was not the first time a fashionable item has been rejected, most notable was the sack dress of the late 50's which was horribly unflattering, and no one bought (Van Rensselaer Thayer 1957, F9). Coco Chanel said of the sack:

> The sack dress… Is made for potatoes or wood – not for women. It's ridiculous, thought up by men designers who wish to make women ugly. It's too easy to make, just up and down with the little fuss at the collar. No one with any sense will wear it. (Van Rensselaer Thayer 1957, F9)

Chanel, the "queen of beige" (F9)—and of chic smart dressing for women—was correct, the sack stayed firmly *on* the rack, as did the midi. The reaction to the midi was particularly vehement however and signaled a real seismic shift in consumer confidence in North America, where once the client had been intimidated by the designer, now there was a new independence. And as the Weinberg fashion business was "Undercapitalized" it was unable to "survive until fashion got back into favor" (Walz & Morris 1978, 220). As was reported in WWD in

1974, in spite of attempts to spin: "as recently as January. 11th[...] Designer Chester said that both the better line and the sportswear division, Chester Now, were shipping and that business was 35 percent ahead for fall." Bluster aside, the ship was sinking, fast, and soon after it was revealed that the business had failed:

> Chester Weinberg Limited. Went out of business Monday after months of rumours and its systematic denials about its imminent demise. Neither Chester nor Sidney Weinberg principles, were available for comment. (WWD 1974, 1)

With "...neither of the Weinberg's available for comment, it could not be immediately ascertained if there were any unfilled orders to be shipped" (21), this would prove to be immaterial, there would be no more orders taken for Weinberg as a designer after 1974. Although a professional blow, it would allow for more personal freedom: "Weinberg had spent many years and many hours in therapy denying his homosexuality, even to himself, before coming out in the mid-1970s, shortly after his label folded" (Campbell 2020, pgh. 6). He would be one of the new generation of Gay men who dared to live openly.

Youthquake: The Advent of AIDS in the Fashion Community

"It's better to look at the sky than live there. Such an empty place; so vague. Just a country where the thunder goes and things disappear."

A designer with a good reputation in the industry, and particularly one in possession of a thorough working knowledge of manufacturing is rarely out of work for long. Weinberg bounced back and was soon designing "cashmere sweaters for Ballantyne, dresses for Jones New York, ready to wear for Hanro". He had "joined the growing army of freelance designers" which was one of the "big developments of the 1970s" and according to Morris he "still had his name on the labels" (Walz & Morris 1978, 220). Chester then went in-house to run CK jeans for his buddy Calvin and rode that wave of success.

Unfortunately, after AIDS hit, that career resurrection would not have been possible. It made Gay men virtually unemployable as designers for a time. The publicist Karen Fortier explained to The New York Times in 1986 that:

> For an industry that has worked hard to be a serious industry and to overcome the stereotypes, it might be difficult to then stand up and say we're very concerned about this disease when everyone knows that the majority of people currently being affected are gay. It's in a way admitting that there's some validity to a stereotype that was not very positive. (Fortier 1986 qtd. in Campbell 2020, pgh. 5)

She was of course talking about AIDS. And although Fortier does not elaborate on why an industry predominately populated by Gay men could be neither "serious" nor "positive", she clearly echoes the hostile climate faced by Gay men in the early 1980's in the fashion industry.

As the brilliant Simon Doonan—who was the chief architect of the extraordinary window displays of Barney's over the past thirty years—recounts in *The Asylum: A Collage of Couture Reminiscences... and Hysteria* (2013):

> Thirty years ago, when AIDS arrived, it hit the fashion industry - my people - like a sledgehammer. Readers d'un certain âge will recall how bleak and ghastly it was. Like me, you can only remember those dark days with a mixture of horror and sadness. To those of you who were not around, I can only say this: you have no idea how lucky you are. one after another, the brightest and boldest succumbed to this horrifying disease (Doonan 2013, 130-131).

He elaborates:

> Our creative pals—some famous, some infamous, most unknown and just starting to hit their stride—perished after being unwittingly affected by the disease of the century. Many died agonizing deaths in the hallways of hospitals without hope or familial support. Back then, in the early days, AIDS really was just like a medieval play. Who is next? Was the question on all our lips (Doonan 2013, 131).

Gossip, innuendo, and subterfuge became the norm. Soon it would be impossible to hide as the fashion ecosystem was devastated:

> Patrick Kelly, Angel Estrada, Isaia, Adrian Cartmell, Clovis Ruffin, Halston and so many more. AIDS decimated a broad spectrum of the fashion universe. Antonio Lopez and Juan Ramos, Tina Chow, Robert Rose, Peter Lester, Tim Hawkins, Sergio Galeotti, Robert Hayes, and Laughlin Barker. photographers too: David Seidner, Barry McKinley, Tony Viramontes, Herb Ritts, Bill King, Steve Arnold, Stevie Hughes, Kenneth McCowan and

Doug Coder...And so many of my window-dresser pals:
Bob Curry, Michael Cipriano, Cliff Murphy, Colin Burch,
Bob Enzo, Steven Di Petrie Talmadge the one-namer, and
so many more. These names are just the tip of the iceberg.
I cannot list everyone. This book would turn into *War and
Peace*. (Doonan 2013, 131)

In "AIDS and the Fashion World: Industry Fears for Its
Health" (1990) Woody Hochswender of the NYT
recounted the terrible toll AIDS was taking on the New
York fashion industry. It was easier to hide at the
beginning, but as it grew worse it was impossible to
contain: "In the beginning, it was hitting the lower
echelon, and it was kind of hush-hush. Then we lost some
major contributors to the industry" (Stolls qtd. in
Hochsender 1990 A.1., pgh. 10). There would be no
escaping what was to come, the fashion industry is
peopled by exactly who were the first to fall from AIDS:
"In this industry, it surrounds you," said a fashion
executive. "It creates a kind of claustrophobic feeling."
(Hochswender 1990 A.1. pgh. 5), namely young,
creative, professional men:

> At a time when the apparel business needs new direction to
> bolster the flagging retail sector, important young
> designers have died. Future stars who might replace them
> have found it difficult to find backers, especially if they
> are young and male. (Hochswender 1990 A.1. pgh. 2)

The issue was reduced to one of "insurability". There is a
policy in the fashion industry called a "key man" which is
a form of life insurance wherein the "beneficiaries are the
investors or partners instead of spouses or family, may
lead to discriminatory screening of designers and
executives." Menswear designer Joseph Abboud related
his experience of one of the requirements for a twenty-

year contract: "I had to take extensive medical tests and sign a release to be tested for AIDS" (Abboud qtd. in pgh. 7). The entire agreement was "contingent on the insurance policy" (7). As more designers died, this led to a red flag of "higher claims activity" Cohen in (Hochswender 1990 A.1., pgh. 8). This affected venture capital, risk management, and even whether new initiatives were launched. A partner in a New York law firm which specializes in insurance cases on the behalf of the insured, stated:

> A fair number of my clients with AIDS have been in the fashion industry. Some have been told by their health insurance companies that their AIDS was a pre-existing condition. I've also consulted with people who thought they were going into business deals, but decided not to go ahead with them because they knew they would test HIV positive. It seems likely that's a very frequent occurrence. (Scherzer qtd. Hochswender 1990 A.1., pgh. 8)

Todd Oldham recalls how testing was required "before concluding negotiations with various potential investors." (8). He stated: "I've taken the AIDS test four times now. They say it's for insurance, but they don't want their money to drop dead in 10 years. It's heartless, but business is business." (Oldham qtd. in Hochswender 1990 A.1. pgh. 8). Civil rights and privacy were pushed aside to secure the bottom line. Like an advancing shadow, AIDS touched the lives of nearly everyone in the fashion industry:

> Beyond the designers who have died, the visual display departments that have been decimated and the sample rooms that have been disrupted, there is the loss of countless unseen people who are the pulse of New York's

second-largest industry: the stylists, illustrators, showroom assistants, makeup artists and hairdressers who not only capture the spirit of fashion but sometimes lead it. (Hochswender 1990, A.1. pgh.1)

The impacts of AIDS "caused designer labels to falter and smaller houses to die, absenteeism and insurance premiums to rise, and venture capitalists to shy away." The men who were the lifeblood of the industry were forced by necessity to become intimately knowledgeable about their medical condition at any given time.

The first men who contracted HIV lived each day in the terror of the unknown, an unknowable threat that they carried within themselves. This virulent illness, and what could be happening at any moment within their own bodies. As "T-4 lymphocytes, a type of white blood cell, are one marker for the degree of infection by AIDS'" this resulted in "How are your T cells? becoming "part of the daily discourse, like the weather and what styles are selling." (Hochswender 1990 A.1., pgh. 4). The personal physical toll was significant. The nature of the illness was that you could be "looking and feeling great one day, and being in the hospital the next." (Pgh. 11). It can't be overstated how stressful living with AIDS was at this time (disclosed or undisclosed). A daily (terrifying and draining) engagement with one's own potential mortality:

I spend an inordinate amount of time and effort staying well," said a fashion publicist who has AIDS. He preferred to be identified, but his supervisors insisted that he not be. "I live with it," the publicist said. "I work with it. I arrange to have less stress. I feel guilty when I'm not pulling my weight". (Hochswender 1990 A.1., pgh. 11)

AZT was not approved as an AIDS medication until 1987, and even then, it was prohibitively expensive to the uninsured (Park 2017). In the 80's the majority of men who contracted AIDS died from it.

However, another casualty was the loss to creativity, in an industry already buffeted by an economic downturn (Hochswender 1990 A.1. pgh. 2). These restrictions and the outright prejudice that fuelled them affected both those working in-house as well as those entrepreneurial young designers looking to start their own brands: "Start-up costs, cash flow, the pace of the seasons - you can't be fighting for your life and have all that on your shoulders." (Fitting qtd. in Hochswender 11). The illness ended careers, stunted initiative, and took some of the best and the brightest. Some of these bright lights were young Black and Latino designers like Willie Smith, Angel Estrada and Patrick Kelly who for the first time in fashion history, were bringing a message of diversity and inclusivity along with their amazing fashion collections.

With the exception of Perry Ellis, companies that lost their head designer to AIDS, just did not last. The Ellis brand however, after losing both the beautiful and gifted Ellis and his partner (in business and life) Laughlin Barker brought in Marc Jacobs to "rejuvenate the business" (9). The brand was thus able to weather the storm:

> Despite the turmoil, some Perry Ellis licenses have had strong sales. "From a business standpoint life goes on and it flourishes," said Claudia Thomas, the president of the company. "We've been devastated by AIDS, savaged by it. On the other hand, we've had increases of 35 percent

per annum for the last two years in our licensing income. (Thomas qtd in Hochswender 1990 A.1. pgh 9)

It was a disaster for Jacobs though as his 1992 grunge inspired looks did not sell well, and he was promptly fired (but he did also win the 1992 CFDA Womenswear Designer of the Year award, so there's that) (Yaeger 2015). The high visibility and notoriety may have helped keep the company afloat during this tumultuous time. Both grunge and Jacobs also perdured, the former as the defining look of the '90's, and the latter quickly becoming a household name, and one of the few openly Gay male designers to achieve success in the early 90's.

The crisis years even precipitated the marketing of a new type of *designer*. Where previously the Gay aesthete was the expert on all things fashionable, the connoisseur with impeccable taste, he was now tainted with the looming spectre of premature mortality and disease, to combat this, now a more virile and unequivocally straight arbiter must be put forth, most notably Christian Lacroix. Susan Faludi in *Backlash, the Undeclared War Against American Women* ([1991] 2009) states that:

> [M]ass media's infatuation with Lacroix involved not only his hyperfeminine clothes but the cult of his masculine personality. Lacroix, who stocked his own wardrobe with Ralph Lauren lord-of-the-manor wear, was eager to market an all-brawn self-image: "primitive people, sun and rough times", he informed the press "this is my real side" (Faludi [1991] 2009, 192).

Faludi recounts how media stories that featured Lacroix were filled with "approving allusions to his manly penchant for cowboys and Matadors." Time magazine in

44

particular included a fashion commentator's fawning tribute: "he looks like Brando; he's pantheroid, cat-like. He is sexy in a way that is absolutely not effete." Faludi nails the root of the desire for this "pantheroid" and "primitive" new type of designer:

> His swagger, and the press's enthusiasm for it, spoke to the real crisis fueling the backlash - not the concern that female professionalism and independence were defeminizing women but the fear that they were emasculating men. Worries about eclipsed manhood were particularly acute in the fashion world, where the perception of a widespread gay culture in the industry had collided in the 80s with homophobia and rising anxieties about AIDS (Faludi [1991] 2009, 192).

The perception of effeminacy, with its connections to homosexuality would in turn always lead straight to AIDS in the late 80's and early 90's.

The only good that came from this era was support for the careers of female designers, who were considered a safer bet and promoted into positions vacated by dead Gay men (Campbell 2016; Hochswender 1990). Donna Karan was able to receive backing from a Japanese group and leave Anne Klein to break out on her own during this time (Campbell 2016). While this is undoubtedly true, in regards to Karan, it also minimizes the strength and power of a designer who was a force that was closely aligned with a maturing movement of emancipation for women—the female professionalism and independence that Faludi identifies. Karan, (like American designers Claire McCardell, Anne Klein, and Diane von Furstenberg before her) knew exactly what women wanted to wear and she provided it. Her singular design vision would have broken through anyway, and unlike Lacroix who crashed and burned, she has stayed the course.

Alive Again: Then as Now

> "We just sort of took up by the river one day, we don't belong to each other: he's an independent, and so am I."

> "You can love somebody without it being like that. You keep them a stranger, a stranger who's a friend."

— Truman Capote, Breakfast at Tiffany's (1958)

There is another photograph of Weinberg in *The Fashion Makers*. Here, he sits on a weathered Muskoka chair [Adirondack for the Americans], the wood grain has been raised by the cumulative impact of many seasons of exposure to the elements. An empty glass beside him, it looks like he has just finished the beverage, as it still appears to hold the vestiges of liquid, maybe soda, maybe vodka, perhaps both. Deeply tanned, he is wearing khakis and a tight tank top, and his head is cocked to one side, almost as if it is necessary to support his hugest of grins. He is clearly amused about something as the smile literally spreads from ear to ear. All around him is verdant foliage. I think this photograph was also taken on Fire Island as I have sat on decks in wild gardens exactly like this one. I can almost hear the sound of wagon wheels on planks, carrying provisions, and friends laughing and catching up as they travel the raised wooden boardwalks transporting them through The Pines

46

community. The animated chatter passes and once again, you hear only birdsong.

The gorgeous excess as well as the natural beauty of The Pines was beautifully chronicled in Tom Bianchi's collection of photographs *Fire Island Pines: Polaroids 1975-1983* (2013), these serve as a testament and visual legacy of his milieu. He created a visual record of his friends and lovers (and these were interchangeable malleable forms of attachment at this time), their lives, and their 1970's world of Queer liberation.

To create his record, Bianchi employed a (then) recently emergent form of photography: the Polaroid. The legend of the creation of the Polaroid was that in December of 1943, Edwin Land was in the desert outside of Santa Fe with his young daughter taking pictures of "The rocky landscape, faintly dusted with snow, [which] would have been brightly lit in dramatic burnt orange and rose rays refracted from an afternoon sun sinking in the sky toward sunset." (8) His daughter asked: "Why can't I see weeks these pictures right now? I don't want to wait." Land pondered this and:

> Instead of dismissively laughing off his daughter's frustration, he shared it, he embraced it, and on the spot, at that moment, he committed himself intellectually to solving his daughter's dilemma. He would figure out a way to create a photographic system— a revolutionary camera and film combination— that would allow images to be viewed immediately after being taken. He would invent "one-step photography" (Fierstein 2015, 8).

Polaroids were fun, they were spontaneous. They brought the images to life as people were waiting. In 1970,

---

47

Charles and Ray Eames made a short film on the SX-70 for Polaroid:

> [A] short promotional documentary about the eponymous camera, showing how it worked, and taking a tour of its circuits, lenses, and moving parts. The Eames connect the camera with toys right from the start: the first demonstration picture is taken of a small boy peering through a set of building blocks (Buse 2016, 34).

One scene from the film the Eames' created, reveals that one of the goals for the SX-70 was: "The removal of the barriers between the photographer and the subject", and later in the film (with remarkable prescience) states that "Thoughtful use can reveal meaning in the flood of images which makes up so much of human life" (Eames 1970), a personalization of the flood of images that had become ubiquitous in 1960's explosion of colour tv, movies and printed magazines.

The quotidian adoption of the polaroid was most notably practiced by Andy Warhol who said of the emergent form: "A picture means I know where I was every minute...It's a visual diary." (Warhol qtd. in Durrant 2015, 12). A technology of self-mirroring (if not reflection) that he thoroughly incorporated into every aspect of his daily life:

> For the last 30 years of his life until his death in 1987, Warhol carried a Polaroid camera to capture every moment of his life and his circle. And unlike most of today's selfie addicted Instagrammers, Warhol's acquaintances - including Dennis Hopper, Mick and Bianca Jagger, Grace Jones and Jack Nicholson—formed a hedonistic good-time gang of the famous, the infamous and the beautiful. (Durrant 2015, 12)

This capturing of "every moment of his life and circle" was also certainly true for the Bianchi project. He had a "good-time gang" all his own. They were photogenic, and they were exhibitionistic, even when they would not allow their faces into the frame for fear of repercussions. The sculpted, muscular torsos thus have the qualities of historic Greek marbles from museums. (Bianchi's crew thankfully all still have penises firmly attached.) But these warriors were ferried over from the mainland, where they worked as "professionally credentialled men, moguls, models, designers, composers, dancers, actors" or were "hunks with no apparent work" (Bianchi 2016, 10). Unlike pristine white marble statues, they had deep tanlines, revealed when they stripped themselves bare in their Dionysian-disco orgies of…well, orgying.

Bianchi states that his camera was given as a "toy" (Bianchi 2016, 4) from a work conference. As a novice photographer the "ease" of image making afforded by the polaroid allowed him to "interact with [his] subjects" he clarifies the ambitions for his work: "I never set out to be a photographer I simply wanted to tell the world that we were here and show them what our world looked like." (4) He describes how the "camera's unique colour systems created painterly images" which were beautiful to him. The camera proved to be a "quick teacher". 4 He then became so consumed by his project that he ended up becoming the second largest consumer of the SX-70 film his camera required...in the world: "Only IBM bought more". (5). His work also has elements of ethnography as he records the intricacies of his milieu, little suspecting how vulnerable and delicate that joyous slice of life perched atop a sandbar overlooking the ocean would soon

---

prove to be. Those halcyon of images of beautiful, doomed men…

Documenting his milieu became a dream book project for Bianchi. Even Warhol himself expressed interested in the project: "he went through the dummy, repeating languidly as he turned the pages, 'That's nice, That's nice. Oh, that's nice. That could be bigger'. That's nice. Reaching the end of the book he said 'I have to go now' he told Bob [Colacello] 'we should do this book'. Turning to me 'Bob will call you'". Bob did indeed call, but "Andy's publisher wasn't keen" (Bianchi 2016, 5). Bianchi then took the project to Sam Wagstaff the illustrious "former museum curator, photo collector and Robert Mapplethorpe's lover/mentor." Bianchi states of the meeting that "Sam gave me invaluable editorial advice...he challenged my editorial choices in a number of cases." (6). Bianchi showed Wagstaff the "secret stash of explicit pictures, a number of which he thought should be included in this book. He suggested I not pull punches". Wagstaff counselled him:

> "Tell me Tom, are we making this book for our mothers? If so, it won't be very interesting. I will grant you the eye. You can compose a picture. But you can't make this book about your ability to compose pictures. That's not interesting. You have one thing no one else has. You have the uncanny ability to take us behind closed doors of you and your friend's lives. Make your book about these people. That will be fascinating hundreds of years from now". (Wagstaff qtd. in Bianchi 2013, 6)

Even with help of the formidable Wagstaff, Bianchi was unable to get the project off the ground, and it would not be long before circumstances and the realities of life would swamp this ambitious art endeavor:

> After knocking on too many more locked doors. I put the photos away in a box. The Pines was Ground Zero as AIDS exploded about that time. That was thirty years ago. A horrific amount of the life recorded in my pictures was consumed in the chaos of the crisis within a few years. I could not have imagined then that my Polaroids would so suddenly become a record of the lost world – my box of pictures a mausoleum, too painful to visit. (Bianchi 2016, 5-6)

He describes one particular reaction to his photographs as he tried to pitch the book: "I've never seen anything like this before. I never managed imagined this kind of intimacy between men." It was an observation from a straight man, he asked "do you think Fire Island is well enough known so gay people know what it is?" The book was not picked up as "marketing...would not risk so much capital on a book so queer." The image in question though was a photograph of "two men in a hammock, one removing a splinter from the foot of the other" (Bianchi 2016, 5). Intimate, sensitive, loving, yet also such a chilling portent of what was to come. The splinter would quickly grow to become a thorn in our collective side, and finally the volley of arrows that felled St. Sebastian. Unknowingly, Bianchi had captured the last, vibrant days of a tragic kingdom.

When Bianchi re-opened his box "decades later", contained inside he "found friends and lovers playing and smiling. Alive again." (Bianchi 2013, 5-6) The rich lifeworld that they had created for themselves was all there beautifully and perfectly documented.

Preserved, and ready for when the world-at-large was finally ready to once again look and engage with these beautiful brave men of the late 70's...*2013*!

Alive Again: Now as Then

There is a Bianchi polaroid of a man taking a shower. He is outdoors, the shower head is set into a flat cedar backing, one that has gone grey from the elements. Along with the cascading water, his beautiful body is simultaneously drenched with sunlight, both of his arms are raised up and his back arched, as if he's just finished lathering up his hair, to wash it with shampoo, or perhaps he's just rinsed it. He's *very* deeply tanned, and his bare bum shows that perfect light outline of where a speedo normally blocked the sun; the colours resemble the contrast between the inside and outside of a freshly baked challah. I would imagine from the light, it is late morning, I can almost smell the coffee mingling with the scent of the ocean; hear the sound of the shower spray. The shower has a barrier that is about mid-chest high, just over this, a vivid strip of the ocean can be discerned in the background, and behind that the horizon just raises up to the heavens. This shower *overlooks* the beach. It is truly a glorious image, and it is also a truly glorious shower. Outdoor showers are one of my favourite things in the world, having your skin exposed to the heat of the sun just as the cold water hits you is a sensation equally bracing and revitalizing. Heaven.

Modern Fire Island is not that different from the days Weinberg knew, and those described by Bianchi:

> The beach stretches to Infinity. The older houses are modest shacks and some, like an early house I rented on Pine Walk, were floated over from the mainland. As the Pines grew, the newer houses took on modern forms, some as imposing cedar mansions designed with the desires of gay men in mind. (Bianchi 2013, 7)

Of course, it is not all soaring beach houses here, there are other houses, some much closer to a rabbit warren of tiny rooms that are shared. The infamous Fire Island "share", big or little is the main means of accessing life at The Pines. Most of the accommodations are rented shares for the entire summer, sometimes two to a room, often four to a room. (Another reason the Meat Rack is so popular no doubt.) Everyone wanting to get out of the city, get away from the urban heat and congestion, and come to this natural, beautiful place. Often bringing with them much of the city, the hustle, the party, the drugs, the hierarchical jostling, that competitive Gay BS, all of it can be found here. Then as now. Such is life. That is not *all* that can be found here, however...

First to Fall

"I want to still be me when I wake up one fine morning and have breakfast at Tiffany's."

— Truman Capote, Breakfast at Tiffany's (1958)

Chester was the first fashion star to fall, the first of many though. His demise was the seismic tremor, the preliminary shock of the terrible times to come. It is unusual [for me anyway,] to write an essay, a legacy-based essay, about a designer I've never actually heard of before. And whose work I have never seen. Weinberg may indeed be "forgotten", but this does not mean that he has left no legacy in his wake. Chester Weinberg, who, as I have now come to learn was a leading New York designer, one who inspired, displayed his work season after season, and was formative to the development of the New York fashion scene. He worked to create a uniquely American aesthetic, one driven by practical concerns:

> I am not interested in reflecting Paris tendencies. I do not want to be known as a trend setter. I design clothes that reflect no age point of view, no seasonal point of view. The clothes are practical. (Weinberg qtd. in Christy 1981, pgh. 2)

A designer who was also driven by the client who wore the fashions be created: "She's intelligent and she's very busy. She's a doer. She has to wear her clothes. Her clothes cannot wear her" (pgh. 7). No diva, he was the "type" of designer who "quietly buzzes in and out of major Manhattan department stores, checking the heavily laden sales racks." always guided by the market, careful to gauge what was ultimately going to sell...or not: "What's left over are all the fads and fancies". Weinberg stated of the leftover dregs he observed: "Even when the price is right, people won't take them" (Weinberg qtd. in Christy 1981, pgh. 5). He also was a keen observer of people, a man who "hovered" in coffee shops to watch and listen: "…getting firsthand impressions about how people interact to each other: 'I see corporate executives sitting at counters talking about careers to the waitresses. They talk to each other as women doing jobs. There's much less separation between people.'". He was in pursuit of a "general camaraderie, the pursuit of people to make real contact with each other" (Pgh. 6). Interesting observations from an interesting man, one who definitely did not design by decree from within the "ivory tower" (pgh. 5). Weinberg was also the first (then) famous fashion personality to die of AIDS, but the latter definitely need not define his final legacy. There is more to this story. What is particularly significant about Weinberg for me is that he also was an educator. The man who, back when he was that "small, wispy boy" from Brooklyn had once envisioned himself running an art department at a school, eventually went back to his alma mater Parson's and tasked himself with guiding and nurturing the careers of future generations of young designers. Through his mentoring and educating he guided and shaped the nascent talents of Donna Karan, Isaac Mizrahi and Marc Jacobs among many, many others (Campbell pgh. 1). To this day, The Chester Weinberg Gold Thimble Award, and the Chester Weinberg Scholarship award (the latter endowed by Klein) help support new design talent as well, so while his name may not be included in the narratives of twentieth century fashion, his influence is still nurturing and growing the designers of the future.

Truman Capote through his alter ego Holly Golightly in *Breakfast at Tiffany's* states "Anyone who ever gave you confidence, you owe them a lot" (1958). We owe Chester Weinberg a lot, he stood up, came out and proclaimed himself a Gay man at a time when there were serious consequences for that honesty. He also died at a time when AIDS was new: all terror and mystery, the gut-wrenching panic of staring into the abyss, that awful impending unknown. It was the stunned reaction to the tragedy of losing so many of his generation, and so swiftly, that catalyzed ameliorative change. (Change effected largely by those men themselves, even as they were gravely ill and dying.) Heroes. I had never heard of him before I researched this essay, but I know now I would have liked to have taught with him, or learned from him, he gave me confidence and I never knew it, I do owe him a lot. Most of all though, what we collectively owe to Chester Weinberg, and to that entire first generation of lost men is to *remember* them. Hold them close.

Figure 11, "Chester Weinberg Dress (1967)" @Mark O'Connell 2021

Reflections on the Ocean

It still does you know, the beach at Fire Island I mean, stretch out to infinity. On the beach at twilight, it captivates as you sit and observe. In a line behind you along the shore, cresting the dunes, the modernist edifices observe the waves crashing in as well, stoic and elegant in their cool modernity.

When temporarily released from academic responsibilities, I am on a semi-permanent quest of looking for those places where earth meets water meets sky most exquisitely. Cuba, Mexico, Northern Ontario, the Outer Banks of the Carolinas, Maine, Martha's Vineyard. I go to these places to reconnect with some essential quintessence of myself. The vitality that gets crusted and covered by the grime and grind of urban living. I had certainly been to Fire Island before but had not spent a lot of time there in the past. Friends have houses there; but for me, it was mostly day trips when I was staying with other friends in the Hamptons. During the summer of 2019, I decided it was time for a deeper dive, I went on my own to *witness*, and to learn.

I found Fire Island is truly a glorious place. From the 1970s through the horrible late 80s, to the resurgence and now present vibrancy of the scene, it is an unbroken continuum. And make no mistake, it is indeed a "scene"; there are still plentiful satyr-like shenanigans going on at the Meat Rack; after the Tea dances of course. The environment, the environs themselves are uniquely beautiful though, and they have an effect on one's psyche. Here, clenched Chelsea queens who don't give anyone a second look in Manhattan offer a friendly hello and a wave in passing on the elevated wooden boardwalks. *Everybody* is friendly here; it is like an R-Rated Disneyland lifted from the pages of Architectural Digest.

I stayed in a spacious and charming mid-century holiday house with retro-chic décor, low teak furniture and objets d'art. Also, floor-to-ceiling windows that looked out onto a cultivated jungle-like garden of flowers and foliage; the house was completely immersed in the greenery. (As I am not a billionaire those sexy, stoic, altogether spectacular modernist beach edifices situated on the shore remained tantalizingly out of reach...not that staying at the cottage was cheap either, lordy!) My host, originally from Brazil, also worked as a caterer and would spontaneously cook the most amazing meals for me. This was a huge plus as the cuisine of The Pines seemed to be more of the egg-white omelette, served with a double espresso variety. People looked at me like I was from Mars when I asked where I could get the best lobster roll?

There were two much younger (gorgeous) guys also staying in the house when I was there. They were lovely fellas, twentysomething young professionals, one a hunky Black man originally from Texas with the face of an angel, the other, a very hairy Midwestern farm boy with piercing blue eyes; I think they had once been a couple but were now besties. They could both easily have been models.

They asked me to come to the nightly Tea dance gathering, or to accompany them to the many parties that

---

they were attending. I said no. They would give me this inquisitive look, heads slightly cocked to one side pondering: "he seems cool, why doesn't he want to go?", they would nod their heads in kindly assurance, almost grandmotherly, beckoning: "Yes, come join us". They did not understand why I was unable to partake in their revelry; I was not going to explain further. It is what it is. They eventually accepted it and went on their very merry way. We would meet at sunset on the pier and catch up. I loved those guys for their lively spirits and their generous natures, they were the essence of Fire Island for me.

Here is the thing about The Pines, there was a space for me even though I chose not to engage with some aspects of the "scene" there. Fire Island offers many alternatives to loud, pumping disco, and men who would like to pump or be pumped...loudly. I will return in the future and no doubt will explore some of that side as well (count on it). Although I no longer debauch, I still actually manage to have fun on occasion. External to the revelry though, is still that the ever-present beauty. I was consistently dazzled by the prismatic light, the sheer magic of the surroundings that took my breath away as I walked aimlessly or went to meet friends at the beach. Coffees in hand, we sat watching the ocean—early morning light playing off the incoming rolling waves— talking, laughing...being.

For this trip, I was after a different sort of "fun", a cerebral engagement as I was also travelling within my thoughts. My dear sister sent me off from Manhattan with a snack for the train and a copy of *Bird by Bird* by Anne Lamott, a yellow post-it note affixed to the cover that said "your beach reading". I read, I wrote, and I reflected;

and every day I went to the beach. I engaged in a sensory way with the environment there, and in a spiritual way with my quintessence. I spread my blanket out under an umbrella and alternated the focus of my thoughts: from chunks of avid consideration of Lamott; writing in a journal; and then drifting off into my deeper realms and communing with the souls of the departed. When things got too hot, I walked down to the ocean, stripped off my little black speedo, tossed it onto the scorching sand and dove naked into the water. Submerged in the glory that is the ocean, that eternal source, giver of life.

Life I love you; *all* is groovy.

Figure 12, "Halston" @Mark O'Connell 2021

Chapter Two: Halston, a Glamorous life

At the Movies

If you ain't got no money take yo'broke ass home

You say: If you ain't got no money take yo'broke ass home

G...L...A...M...O...R...O...U...S, yeah
G...L...A...M...O...R...O...U...S

We flying the first class

Up in the sky

Poppin' champagne

Livin' my life

In the fast lane

And I won't change

For the glamorous, oh the flossy flossy

Fergie "Glamorous" track 7, *The Dutchess* (2007)

There is a Saturday Night Live skit where Nora Dunn's (very) regional cable TV host (and former model "thank you") Pat interviews a fashion designer; one brilliantly played by Phil Hartman. She calls him Roy, he corrects her: "Halston". She asks questions about a deal that he made, a merger, and subsequent licensing issues. He tries to avoid answering directly and thus preserve his dignity. Finally, she states in a friendly midwestern twang "but there was Halston aquarium gravel at Walgreens". The sketch was very funny, but it also encapsulated many of the commonly held "truths" about the Halston legend. These include the omnipresent lit cigarette, the turtleneck; semi-absurd posturing, and *that voice*: a layered cocaine and loaded-ashtray-inflected parody of a posh East Coast accent (think Thurston and Lovey Howell coming upon some cannibals in Gilligan's Island: "*Heavens*, a Yale Man!"). Also, there is (always) that one terrible deal.

There are few other designers who could be so easily mocked in the mainstream. Mainly, because people just don't know who they are, or they don't possess vivid mediagenic personalities. Halston was a singularity and was so easily parodied because he was such a recognizable personality. He was *the* flamboyant, self-important gay designer. Even now, thirty years after his death, you would be hard-pressed to find a designer that could be put up for similar ridicule on SNL. Armani? A famous name, not a person. YSL, Chanel, Prada are all just logos on purses. Ralph Lauren and Tommy Hilfiger come across as skilled business managers when they describe their product (zzz). Donna Karan, Bill Blass, Oscar de La Renta, Claire McCardell, Charles James? Wonderful designers all, but I'm not sure I could single them all out in a photograph. Michael Kors? Nope. Karl Lagerfeld is really the only other remote possibility. Yet, SNL could confidently pillory Halston because all of Middle America knew *exactly* who he was.

64

I had not planned to write about Halston, not in any substantive way anyway because to me he was always a punchline. I was certainly aware of him in the early 1980's but it was always as a joke. Running around the world with his group of Halstonettes, adjusting that turtleneck layered under the ultrasuede safari jacket while he snapped for someone else to pick up the Louis Vuitton matching luggage. Of course, his importance to fashion history, and his very high profile, warrants inclusion in fashion narratives, but at the end of someone else's piece, or as an admonitory preface to another artist whose body of work and design or overall legacy has better perdured. Everything I read about his career, and the later descriptions from corporate flunkies who had been at war with him, painted him as an unpleasant, over the top, angry screaming Queen. This all resulted in a parodic assemblage that made me think that he just wasn't someone I was particularly moved to *think* about let alone devote the time to write about. Two recent documentaries, a miniseries and my subsequent viewing of Halston archival footage has caused me to reconsider my previously held opinions, and with it revise my understanding of Halston himself.

Documentary One: *Halston*

Frédéric Tcheng's recent documentary: *Halston* (2019), offered me an opportunity to contemplate the legend: equal parts glamorous and disastrous. Tcheng knows his fashion, and is a top-notch documentarian; as he has previously demonstrated in the extraordinary Diana Vreeland documentary *The Eye Has to Travel*, as well as the sublime *Dior & I*. I was therefore excited to see what he would make of Halston. Some of the vantage points that contributed to the success of *Dior & I*, can be seen in Halston; contrasting the corporate with the *petits mains* for example, as Tcheng conducts some interviews with Halston's former workroom staff. This is an important aspect of any fashion film, as no one produces a successful line of clothing alone. However, where *Dior & I* sticks to the facts and flows of the Parisian couture house, and the warm camaraderie of the atelier contrasts so effectively with the brittle loneliness of Raf Simons (who wisely let little of his personal domain be included); *Halston* instead slips into artifice, and even superfluous, jarring re-enactments to tell a tale that ultimately is not really about the subject.

Also, unlike his treatment of la Vreeland and Raf Simons' brief tenure at Dior, both of which were skillfully shot and edited to seem to flow effortlessly from one interview onto another, scene by scene revealing the story—a virtuoso skill as creating an "effortless" documentary is anything but—Tcheng with *Halston* seems more concerned with creating his own stylish film than honestly exploring what his subject was truly about. Where the angst-ridden Simons was singularly focused on his design work (to the exclusion of humour and few personal revelations), and thereby lent his persona easily to the story of mounting his first collection for Christian Dior; the legacy of Halston bridles and chafes at the external impositions of Tcheng's overly directive narrative constructions.

———

66

With *Halston* Tcheng seems intent on telling a premonitory story of fashion business in America, supplying various corporate talking heads who bloviate ad nauseum about the least interesting aspect of fashion: the transactional. From toasters to investment bonds, and yes even with fashion, the corporate bottom line is to deliver lucrative dividends to investors, end-of-story. Tcheng's interviews with the tedious bean counters and boorish middle-managers who facilitate these efforts certainly support his film's narrative, but none of it is very interesting. It is as if Tcheng has never been exposed to American corporate systems. Does anyone not know that the bedrock of big business is built on structural dominance, profit and subjugation? All in the pursuit of maximized ROI. Like a biological function, corporatist capitalist systems certainly need to be in place for the survival of the fashion line, but after listening to these odious ignoramuses self-justify, whinge and prevaricate, someone needed to just pull the chain and flush. There was far too much time given over to these luddites, and at the expense of what was really magical and special about Halston: *the clothes*.

Also, Tcheng doesn't consult anyone from the (then or now) world of fashion journalism or scholarship. Instead, he uses poor Tavi Gavinson as a fictionalized quasi-archivist-cum-gopher: "Who am I?" she asks "just someone working in the archives. nobody important for our story really", this is a remarkably stupid and reductive line of dialogue. Her "role" simultaneously manages to trivialize both Gavinson *and* the important profession of librarian/archivist. (A skilled professional designation that is the bedrock of all rigorous fashion research.) Gavinson became famous for her penetrating eye, and ability to contextualize fashion within the contemporary fashion milieu (starting when she was just twelve); having her spout fatuous clichés like "when it rains it pours" while she rediscovers "lost" archival footage was a waste of any potential insight she could bring to a modern analysis of Halston's oeuvre. And as she was born six years after Halston died, I for one, would be very interested in the contextualizing potential of her analyses.

This lost opportunity is compounded by the fact that there is an actual trained archivist and scholar included in the documentary: Fred Dennis, Senior Curator of Costume Collections at The Museum at FIT. As FIT has the finest (and largest) museum collection of Halston originals, there was a major lost opportunity here. The Dennis interview could easily have been expanded to supply a far more satisfying exegesis of the entire Halston oeuvre. This also could have framed a more edifying and accurate representation of the vital role of a trained archivist. Instead, Tcheng wastes valuable screen time focusing on his fictitious researcher as she winds and rewinds old VHS footage. Ho-hum.

Tcheng has crafted his own story, one replete with film noir jazz trumpets and superfluous, subjective simulations. The result is a very uneven assemblage, a contrived and at times boring documentary that telegraphs the ending (which everyone already knows) and misses what was really magical about Halston. Quite a feat, as it takes some work to make a life *that* celebrity studded, categorized by high living and over the top gorgeousness into such a dreary, and dull little morality tale. Although the descriptions and footage of Halston's garments are the highlight of this film, they are too few and far between. Thus, Tcheng was unable to really capture what the true significance of his subject. His is not the only documentary treatment of Halston, however.

Documentary Two: Ultrasuede

In a frankly strange documentary called *Ultrasuede* (2010) Whitney Sulder-Smith sports oversized aviator sunglasses, bombs around Manhattan in a vintage 1970's Trans Am and spends far too much time talking about himself (who?) and inserting himself into the narrative (who cares?). In spite of these gratuitous and unwarranted intrusions, he actually manages to piece together a compelling picture of the rise and sad downfall of the Halston empire. Sulder-Smith's entrée into the Halston mythology, was rooted in a particular fascination with Studio 54 and disco nightlife; and through this came to alight upon Halston as a subject to illuminate his subject further. It is odd (brazen?) to have someone auto-ethnographizing a topic of which he knows next-to-nothing. However, in his search for Halston, he has access to some pretty high-powered talking heads who can (and do) deliver the goods.

Sulder-Smith asks poorly researched questions of highly knowledgeable people in the field of fashion, and of others who seem selected purely for their celebrity face value. With a bull in a china shop glee, he careens through his interviews with Liza, Anjelica Huston, Pat Cleveland...and Billy Joel (why?) Our documenteur smirks and his raised-eyebrow debauched private-school-boy amusement inflects everything he records; it is all obviously rather droll and inconsequential for him. He interrupts, shifts topics, and asks awful, inappropriate questions at times. He also lecherously ogles models and makes jokes about penis size. Although he does not seem to have much of a grasp of fashion history—for which he is sternly reprimanded by the wonderful Andre Leon Talley—through his interviews he actually, inadvertently, presents many solid reasons for Halston to be included in the annals of fashion history.

Probably because of his overwhelming awkwardness and ineptitude Sulder-Smith actually ends up coming across as somewhat endearing; an idiot-savant who eventually provides a better documentary than the far more skilled and fashion-knowledgeable Tcheng. The key is that Sulder-Smith is able to offer an accurate engagement with a key element of the Halston mystique: debauched hedonistic nightlife. (A life he seems to know intimately as he appears in one scene with what looks like a prominent hickey.) So perhaps he is a better auto-ethnographizer of his subject than I had initially given him credit for?

The Soft Seventies and the Single Seam Dress

"From the moment that I started I always had success and I always had fun…and one thing always led to the other"

———

(Halston 1979 qtd. in Videofashion 2009).

What gets lost in the legend of Halston is who he was as a designer, as a creative, and as a person. For the record, Halston's innovations were no less than the definition of a uniquely American casual chic during the 1970's. This is not hyperbole, he really did it. Born in Des Moines, Iowa, Halston's childhood was a peripatetic existence moving around from Lake of the Ozarks, Kentucky, Missouri and finally settling in Indiana. Like fellow Queer icon James Dean, once Halston got out of Indiana, he never looked back. "I only lived in Iowa for about 5 minutes you know" Halston says tartly to an interviewer trying to get him to elucidate his past, "There is no home in Iowa" (Halston qtd. in Tcheng 2019) he adds, shutting down any further discussion…permanently. Fueled by creativity and ambition Halston rose and rose until he dominated his industry, paralleling a rise in global power and confidence for America itself. Halston struck down the "country bumpkin" notion of North American fashionable display:

> In the "old New York" described in the novels of Edith Wharton, respectable ladies stored away their precious Paris fashions for two years, as appearing in the latest looks was considered dangerously "fast". Ever since, America had remained the Cinderella of the fashion world, a country bumpkin who needed European designers to show her what to wear. Halston's aesthetic was the revolution it had been waiting for. (Hilton 2019, Pgh. 2)

Halston took Cinderella to the ball. From Jackie's inaugural pillbox onward he always "had success" (Halston interview in Videofashion 2009) and he enjoyed it. He was uniquely American, and designed for a pre-globalized fashion industry:

> [H]e studied at the School of the Art Institute of Chicago, before opening his first millinery boutique in 1953. Four years later he moved to New York with a clientele that already included movie stars such as Kim Novak and Deborah Kerr. In 1961, he designed the pillbox hat Jackie Kennedy wore for the presidential inauguration. Fresh, simple and playful, it allied perfectly with the woman whose style became part of a new American mythology (Hilton 2019, Pgh 2).

He made the chic bunny mask that Candace Bergen wore to Katharine Graham and Truman Capote's Black & White ball, as well as many others seen at that exclusive 1966 evening at the Plaza.

CANDACE BUNNY

Halston was such a success in the 60's that he had his own dedicated hat boutique installed en situ at Bergdorf Goodman; with a department of one hundred milliners and twelve salespeople. He was also the first designer "personality" promoted by them. According to Liz Smith:

> He began in New York working for Lily Dache, cultivated the world's greatest names (Garbo, Barbara Hutton, Marlene Dietrich) during his years at Bergdorf and opened his own salon to raves in 1968. He was fashion's golden boy when I first met him - full of charm, urbanity, generosity, sophistication and an arch wit (Smith Pgh. 5).

For Halston, the work of creating the easy draped elegance he was known for "began with refusal" (Hilton 2019, pgh. 3). He discarded superfluity and clutter: "I don't like pockets that don't work or buttons that don't button anything..." (Halston 1979 qtd. in Videofashion 2009). He also focused on value over trend: "It's much better for the client to have clothes that you can wear until they almost wear out, and don't become faddy or the fashion of the moment" (1979 qtd. in Videofashion 2009). He had a beautiful eye for colour which popped, as he was such a minimalist otherwise. "He eradicated all extraneous detail in favour of an absolute purity of line. His pieces are ridiculously easy to wear, streamlined, graceful, yet powerfully sexy" (Hilton 2019, Pgh 3). This is not an easy combination to navigate, as it takes virtuosic skill to simultaneously embody grace, purity, sex and *comfort*.

Figure 13 "Halston Gown" @Mark O'Connell 2021

He used beautiful, draped fabrics that caught the light, hammered satins, beading, a gorgeous triple weight cashmere. Everything *moved*: "No zippers just get in and out over your head" (North qtd. in Tcheng 2019). I well remember from fashion school that bias cut chiffon is a nightmare to work with as it continues to reshape even as it hangs. You therefore have to re-hem a bias gown a week or so after it is finished, sometimes more than once. His amazing one piece of fabric gowns required patterns that look like "Cuisinart blades" (Dennis qtd. in Tcheng 2019). Diaphanous does not correspond with unexacting, his works are technical marvels.

Halston was already an industry veteran when he made the break from Bergdorf Goodman to set up his own fashion house. He knew his fabrics, and how to work with the mills. Halston also was a textile innovator, bringing in the widespread use of Ultrasuede, a Japanese microfibre that provided easy care and cleaning. The Ultrasuede shirtdress went on to become the quotidian day uniform of the fashionable Northeastern society matron for a spell during the late 1970's. He developed one of the most successful fragrances in history (one that didn't even feature his name on the bottle). His bottle was sculptural and had the same elegance as a Tiffany silver cuff (in fact, designer of the bangle Elsa Peretti also designed his bottle). He collaborated with Martha Graham on dance costumes which elevated his gift for movement and body-focused design to its apogee.

PERETTI CUFF

Halston also helped open the door to a more comprehensive beauty aesthetic by booking Black models. You can look at footage from his first independent runway show for his eponymous label in 1968 and he has cast Black models from the very beginning. Tcheng provides footage of legendary Somali supermodel Iman's very first fashion show ever, at Halston's Madison Av. atelier. Alva Chinn and Pat

Cleveland were perennial favorites–both on and off the runway as the latter two were favoured Halstonettes. If you review the footage of his runway shows, there is representation and a concomitant, clear affirmative statement about diverse beauty that wasn't reflected in other fashion media of the era (or even consistently today).

He was also funny! There are clips form the 1972 Cody Fashion Awards where Halston staged a "talent" show with his favorite models. Described as a "An Onstage Happening by Andy Warhol", model and Halstonette Karen Jorgensen happily played her clarinet as all hell broke loose, as the *New York Times* reported:

> Instead of mannequins sedately modeling Halston's famous flowing matte, jersey dresses, platinum-blond actress Donna Jordan tap-danced wildly, then flung up her Halston outfit to reveal that she had nothing on underneath. She was followed by a Warhol star, Jane Forth, who lugged her baby son to the footlights, and left him there, presumably hunting for his bottle. Next, some nameless girl performed a mediocre juggling act, while ex-model China Machado, wearing a Halston caftan, attempted to play the bongos. (Bosworth 1973, 320)

All culminating with the remarkable finale of Pat Ast coming out of a cake warbling "Happy birthday to me"… fabulous. Fabulous! The *New York Times* also described the reaction of the black-tie top-tier fashion crowd:

> [T]he audience expressed confusion and shock. Was Halston putting the Establishment on—or putting Seventh Avenue down? Nobody seemed to know, but nobody approved, and they said so. (320)

Halston's rebuttal was:

> I refuse to be taken so seriously…It was fun and a camp.
> God, I hate pretensions! If it shook some people up,
> goody. … I loved it. The whole thing freaked me out.
> (Halston qtd in Bosworth 1973, 320).

Goody indeed, unfortunately, this refreshing antipathy towards pretension would not last much longer.

Halston's use of Pat Ast, a Warhol "superstar", was particularly significant as she was plus size and not conventionally beautiful. Halston put her on his runways anyway and employed her in his Madison Av. showroom. He was questioned about this, queried if he was once again making fun of fashion. To which he replied that it would only be true if he considered Ast's appearance funny which he unequivocally did not (Halston qtd. in Videofashion 2009). His attitude is prescient, progressive and aligns with one of his career ambitions, which was to dress "all women". (An idea that has not entered the fashion zeitgeist until very recently.)

Altogether, his was a unique vision, albeit a solitary one: "I usually do my creative exercise quite alone" (Halston qtd. in Videofashion 2009). His designs and silhouettes were certainly guided by the larger zeitgeist, but his aesthetic, approach and execution does not waver. As he stated:

> I dress people from all over the world, but I'm a New York
> designer I don't have anything to do with the European
> cuts or European style or anything else because it's quite a
> different country (1984 qtd. in Videofashion 2009)

Can you name a contemporary fashion product that is not designed for simultaneous rollout in panoplied global markets? I can't. From the Faubourg Saint-Honoré to Rodeo Drive, modern fashion by necessity must travel. Not Halston, he designed for New Yorkers, 1970's New Yorkers to be specific. Glittering societal swans who navigated a dangerous and garbage strewn urban environment, equal parts dystopic and decadent. If he was also eventually a success with the international fashion elite, it was only because they came to him.

In fact, they *all* came to him, for a time anyway. From Jackie Kennedy onwards, he fostered a symbiotic relationship with female beauty and power:

> ...[I]t was so great to see him with all these beautiful women, like Marina Schiano and Naomi Sims, and then suddenly being in love with all these movie stars. He admired Liza Minnelli and Elizabeth Taylor like crazy...(Cleveland qtd. in La Ferla & Trebay 2019, pgh. 22)

It was not a one-sided love affair though, as these dazzling women needed Halston as well: "Elizabeth was getting older and wasn't dressing well. And Liza needed someone to dress her up and make her shinier. He made them both modern" (Cleveland qtd. in La Ferla & Trebay 2019 pgh. 22). From Betty Ford to Bianca Jagger, he created an easy, elegant, comfortable iconography in which they could inhabit. Truly he helped make them all "modern".

He could do this successfully because he produced quality: "You're only as good as your standard, as good as what you do" (Halston 1981 qtd. in Videofashion

2009). When you watch the runway shows in the Olympic tower aerie [with only eight models, he certainly wasn't opulent with his casting] you are witnessing a fantasy made real. An American fantasy that was elevated well above the good teeth, athleticism, and shiny haired chestnuts that had hitherto defined North American beauty. Halston's vision was an exclusive one, but it was also a sexy, confident, and liberating one. The footage of Pat Cleveland twirling and whirling away on the catwalk, makes you dizzy, as she joyfully trails vaporous wings of gossamer chiffon; the spires of St. Patrick's Cathedral can be seen directly outside the window. It is breath taking and evokes such a clear vision of 1970's New York chic. Adding further poignancy are those symbols of 70's peak modernism: the World Trade Centre towers that could also be seen from his celestial runway at that time. Who would have ever imagined how quickly it could *all* come crashing down?

Everybody loves a winner, and unfortunately Halston is conversely viewed as the all-time fashion loser and is therefore despised. As a result, the laurels and attributions have been stripped from his legacy and bestowed upon others. The simple, shirtdress staple, a product for which Diane von Furstenberg is credited, she herself attributes to Halston's innovation. (Although to be fair, DVF effectively embodied that ethos as she was her own best model for the 1970's work/glamour/motherhood conflation that the wrap dress came to signify.) East Coast, elegant, minimalist simplicity, the banner that Calvin Klein and Michael Kors have become the bellwether for was originated by Halston. Flowing body conscious minimalist evening looks with a sculptural statement bangle or a glint of shining metal are attributed to Tom Ford, yet Ford himself vocally credits his predecessor. Although Halston was at the vanguard of all that societal change and fashion iconography, like a proscription in ancient Rome where the named proscribed is murdered and the ancestral household stripped of all valuable possessions, the glamorous legacy of Halston has been ransacked. Of all his innovations though, it is the movement that really stands out for me, and I will return to this idea of beautiful gesture in the conclusion.

The Definition of

G...L...A...M...O...U...R

The word most associated with Halston according to those interviewed who attempt to elucidate his character, is that ever-elusive term: "glamour". A ubiquitous word that when one is called upon to substantiate, conversely becomes ever-more nebulous. What is "glamour" exactly? For all of its accessibility, it is very difficult to actually define. It conflates with so many other terms that can be equated with glamour, but are themselves mutually exclusive: stylish, sexy, elegant, languid, beautiful, tragic, rich, magnetic, aloof, siren, swan, sex goddess, mystique. Stephen Gundle, in his book *Glamour: A History* (2013) summarizes the challenge of defining glamour:

Glamour has talismanic qualities. It has a sparkle and glow about it that enhance people, objects, and places to which it is attached. Yet despite the ubiquity of the term, glamour is notoriously difficult to define. Everyone has an idea of what they think it means but few know where it comes from and why it is so tantalizing to so many (Gundle 2013, 2).

Veteran fashion theorist Elizabeth Wilson has written on the topic as well in *A Note on Glamour* (2007). She covers a massive chronological and philosophical spectrum: the Romantic movement and Gothic fiction; Walpole, Keats, Byron; the rise of the dandy; Baudelaire in France; Georg Simmel's ideas of glamour as a force field; spells and witchcraft; femme fatales; Dracula as a metaphor for syphilis; Garbo and Dietrich; 50s glamour created by Dior and Balenciaga; the glamour of evil: the moors murderers; Julia Kristeva and the abject; Cindy Sherman; Tracy Emin; Lady Diana and AIDS; Andy Warhol and the glamour of madness, drugs and debutantes; the Lower East Side heroin chic aesthetic of Nan Goldin; Alexander McQueen; and finally the Roland Mouret galaxy dress...[Puts down article for a moment, wipes brow]. Definitely thought-provoking and clearly speaks to the multiplicity of meanings glamour offers up.

Within her kaleidoscopic vision, Wilson still manages to narrow her focus enough to try to hammer the nail in the coffin of the notion of contemporary glamour though: "Glamour was beginning to be eaten away by vulgarity. For a time it had a symbiotic relationship with the mass media, but eventually the mass media invented celebrity as its democratic alternative" (Wilson, 2007, 101), and sharply contrasts glamour with celebrity: "Celebrity is open, shameless, vulgar, in-your-face, *nouveau riche.*

The feelings elicited by celebrity have more to do with envy, malice, greed, and *Schadenfreude* than with longing, admiration or aspiration" (101). However, Wilson fails to recognize that glamour has always slinked along that thin line between elegance and vulgarity, the Belle Epoque courtesans and actresses Wilson mentions used their beauty and glamour tropes to broadcast their sexual allure and power…equally shameless. Old money has never been glamorous—elegant and chic at times—but never flashy and certainly not sexy. Glamour always has a price tag, and it is awarded to the highest bidder.

Carol Gould in her article *Glamour as an Aesthetic Property of Persons* (2005) makes the necessary split between glamour and charisma when attempting to define the term. And notes they are etymologically opposite: "'Charisma,' in Greek, means something like favored by the gods, and it conveys a sense of power to change or lead others, a confidence, a sort of radiance. It conveys the aura of light. 'Glamour' is associated with darkness, witches, the occult, that is, the hidden" (Gould 2005, 237). She also makes the interesting observation that children are not glamorous, and then expands on this by saying glamour is a function of a complex psyche. She explores the ontological and philosophical aspects in depth:

> [T]o say that glamour draws from a symbolic field is not to say that it is ontologically dependent on the third party responses of others; rather it is to say that the elements with which one embodies glamour are found in symbolic field of one's own culture (Gould 2005, 245).

However, Gould gets confusing when she sets out to define "true" and "false" glamour and starts to apply these judgments wholesale. For example, when a person does not choose to be glamorous, they are therefore, somehow truly glamorous, and conscious efforts to be glamorous are considered false. She also offers problematic statements like: "False glamour has a transparency. True glamour is a fluent mode of self-expression" (Gould 2005, 245)...says who? Gould's definition of "true glamour" seems closer to a notion of natural grace: "True glamour, being more subtle, flows gracefully from a person's own interior mode of experience" (243). Although glamour certainly requires poise, I would argue that grace is actually the antithesis of glamour. Closer to mystique perhaps, glamour is hard won and adopted, it is not innate.

There appears to be a dichotomy between coded artifice and unique individuality in the appeal of glamour. The adoring public of glamorous figures also have a rapacious appetite for scandal and are constantly looking for cracks in the façade. In *The Second Sex* Simone de Beauvoir talks about the how quickly the glamorous construction can fall apart:

> She is a victim of accidents: a drop of wine falls on her dress, a cigarette burns it; and so the creature of luxury and parties who smilingly struts around the living room disappears: she turns into the serious and hard housewife; suddenly one discovers that her toilette was not a bouquet of flowers, fireworks, a gratuitous and perishable splendour destined to generously light up an instant: it is an asset, capital, an investment, it demands sacrifices; it's loss is an irreparable disaster. (de Beauvoir 1949, 579)

The glamour construct is a staged moment of perfection; but there can be no translation into reality for these goddesses. Glamour is a form of camouflage. It obscures even as it seduces, yet we know what is behind the glamour mask: it is a person, flesh and blood, worried about revealing a self, a true self.

The Ryerson Image Centre (RIC) in Toronto recently mounted an exhibition exploring the at times conflicting constructs of glamour: *Burn with Desire*. The images on display were not just standard pin-ups and studio portraits of Hollywood stars, these are included of course, but there was also much on display to contrast these classic visual iconographies.

Some basic elements used to construct the image of "glamour" can be identified throughout the gallery: it is a performed function, it is expensive, and it alters the basic appearance of the person who is being photographed. Once these basics are established however, the discourse on glamour tends to go into free fall, and the real interest of an exegesis begins.

One visual theme that runs through the exhibition is the consistency of representation of the "glamorous". Glamour codes are readily identifiable: highly stylized lighting, burnished skin, heavy makeup with a defined dark lip, jewels, revealing gowns made from lustrous fabrics, and an overall implied sexual availability. There is a polytpych of *Vanity Fair* magazine Oscar issue covers that illustrate this...*beautifully*. Viewed individually, the various famous actresses are easily recognizable albeit sumptuously put together for their portraits. As the viewer backs up and views the entirety of their images en masse however, the homogeneity of their presentation quickly becomes apparent. A reductive shell has been applied unilaterally. Everyone playing the game so the images will sell, and exalted celebrity status can be maintained. They are all in fact, from a distance, interchangeable.

Another thing that can be gleaned from the exhibition is that the accoutrements of this performance (furs, gowns made from beautiful fabrics and jewels, hair and make-up) costs money. There is a constructed, calculated foundation to glamour. Clearly, performing celebrity is a function of maintaining celebrity. The creation of glamour includes hair stylists, make-up, and a jet set lifestyle, none of which comes cheap. Modern glamorous women who are famous for simply being famous have had to use these expensive props to propel themselves into the glamoursphere, and to remain there. There is a humorous art piece in the RIC exhibition by American artist Barbara Kruger that features Kim Kardashian, one that cleverly comments on this manifestation of celebrity-qua-celebrity. The piece consists of a diptych with Kruger's distinctive bold text spelling out the words "It's all about you, I mean me, I mean you" covering Kardashians naked body. The reality show siren stares back at the viewer, neither deferential nor confrontational, the self-possession is paramount, however. There is a self-referential irreverence about the piece that is very funny, and both artist and glamorous reality-show megastar are united in telling this particular joke.

The work of Mickalene Thomas is included in the exhibition as well and provides a refreshing counterpoint with an alternate offering of the "glamorous", offering a beauty aesthetic that uses lush settings, and patchworked textured fabrics to frame the singularity of her beautiful Black models, and thereby disrupts the conformity of the manufactured glamour seen elsewhere in the gallery spaces.

The focal point where all of the visual tropes and thematic elements of glamour converge (in the exhibition and in *life*) is Marilyn Monroe, and the RIC exhibition nails this as the show opens and ends with her iconic images; with the entire first room devoted to her iconic persona. Marilyn is the intersection of all of the conflicting elements of glamour: stellar yet earthy, the siren, the aspiring intellectual who read and studied with Strasberg, the woman-child from underprivileged circumstances who climbed the heights of stardom, yet also battled mental illness and was ultimately in such despair that she took her own life. Marilyn embodies the many conflicting elements of glamour, uniting them into one iconoclastic icon.

There is a wall of Andy Warhol silkscreen prints. An Avedon portrait snapped between glamour shots when the camera catches an exhausted off moment. There is also a series of photos from the 1962 Golden Globes taken a few months before she died, during which Monroe was followed around by a photographer; in some she is ethereal bathed in limelight, others she is definitely a normal woman, drink in hand and having a laugh. Some of the photos are flattering, some not so much. There are also the staged "candid" publicity photos from early in her career on exhibition, she is reading, and the prop (a book) speaks to her true nature, as Marilyn was both bright and intelligent. There are also images from the day of her funeral: crowded with fans clamoring for one last look at their fallen goddess; sad, just another ordinary early 1960's Los Angeles afternoon, the antithesis of glamour.

Aside from Marilyn though, these glamorous women were uniformly *tough*. For all of the sensuality and allure of the RIC images, there is very little vulnerability to be discerned. Certainly, glamour is not gamine, of the many things that glamour is, nice seems pretty low on the list. Some paparazzi photos of Natalie Wood are included in the RIC show, Wood herself had a very sweet persona, but the truly glamorous figure in those photos is actually her then-fiancé: Warren Beatty. Beatty used a combination of sartorial style, the West Coast lifestyle, and his position at the centre of cool and influential circles to fuel his fame. A nascent manifestation of the use of the "trappings" of style and luxury to sell a personal, branded identity-as-product. In a similar way to this, Halston too was wholly "glamorous", and created a personal persona that helped drive the fashionable enterprise that bore his name.

CORPORATE: 1973-1984

Halston is not remembered for his glamorous persona now though, he is only remembered for (cardinal sin of New York) making a bad deal. (And what a bad deal!) Warhol in his notorious (albeit interminable) diaries muses about what went wrong with Halston's license and marketing agreements, and how he himself could avoid the same fate. As Halston himself stated:

It became a different world from what it was when I started. By the end, you almost had to be a lawyer or an accountant to survive as a designer. Just one word in a contract can change everything, and it did for me (Halston qtd. in Darnton 1990, pgh 10).

Here is the deal: in 1973 David Mahoney of Norton Simon bought everything associated with the ascendant atelier of Halston, including the rights to this newly famous name... "forever". Henceforth, Halston would be branded on furniture; car interiors, carpets; shoes; two men's fragrances; an entire cosmetics line; luggage; carpets; sheets; bags; gloves; sunglasses. Halston felt that he had to individually design everything that was being licensed, if it had his name on it, it was his. This would be his downfall. Thus, what Halston is forever remembered for is the associated perils of licensing.

However, it must be noted that the "bad deal" worked amazingly well for a very long time. Without it, Halston may well have stayed put in his walkup on Madison Av. The corporate collaboration paid for the soaring, mirrored, Olympic Tower showroom that overlooked St. Patrick's cathedral, the legendary townhouse, the beachfront getaway in Montauk; all of the accoutrements of lux. Which for Halston also involved a colossal volume of orchids, and many lavish expensive parties. The deal also paid for what must be the loveliest, most expensive workroom in the history of fashion.

Production samples and Halston originals were not farmed out to contractors in New Jersey. No sir. The workroom was set up right there in Olympic tower as well, and a beautiful view was provided for the behind-the-scenes workforce. That definitely is not common practice in fashion manufacturing (then or now). For with fashion ateliers (akin to restaurants) the design and presentation of the customer-facing aspects of the business (versus the preparation spaces) are very different (to the detriment of the latter). From Maxim's to Le Cirque, velvet drapes and plush banquettes quickly give way to stainless steel and plastic tubs of assorted ingredients once you push through those swinging doors into the kitchen. Not so at Halston's. Apparently, the craftspeople employed by Halston wept when they first saw the Olympic Tower space where they were to practice their craft. The fact that he included them this way, speaks to the profound depth of understanding and care, *love*, Halston felt for his employees.

JC Penny was what caused this glittering kingdom in the sky to come crashing down. In 1982, a one-billion-dollar five-year deal with the popular department store mega-chain was signed by Halston. Halston III was to be the third phase in the ascendant arc of his success, first the millinery, then the haute lux fashion house, and finally the lucrative volume afforded through selling all across America. It was the largest fashion deal that had ever been made at that time, and it was Halston's gateway to the high volume, mass profits that can only be accessed through mass market offerings. However, after the autumn of 1983, everything started to ravel and fray at the edges.

The down-market JC Penney associations caused a tsunami of negative consequences for the Halston brand. Apparently, on his way home from dinner, Ira Neimark president of Bergdorf Goodman drove past banners for the JC Penney Halston III launch that were hanging outside the American Museum of Natural History and quickly became apoplectic. He ordered that all of Halston's merchandise be cleared out of Bergdorf's (Tcheng 2019) that very night! This purge was deadly, because it is the cachet of the high end that sells the highly lucrative ready to wear. First Bergdorf Goodman then other high-end stores quickly followed by cutting back orders. The bloom was off the rose.

The wholesale dumping of the top-tier product range was compounded by the fact that the quotidian Halston III line just did not sell. America is a very large place and tapping into the mass-market there is how massive fortunes are made. Halston's deal with JC Penny, was his way of connecting the common market of fashion retail with the coveted aesthetic of his elite strata of New York ultra-rich. Middle America could now proudly saunter down Museum Mile. Unfortunately, refined, elegant, Park Avenue good taste is not always synonymous with a lively sense of personal style. Self-control and social rigidity are encoded in the politics of representation that manifest in ladies-who-lunch visual aesthetics, a sartorial conformity that does not play well in Peoria. It didn't for Halston anyway.

The disconnect was that mass market tastes rarely align with those of the elite. The two worlds live such different lives and require vastly different things from their wardrobes. For all of the bravado found in Halston's statements that he wanted to dress every woman in America—fatally for the launch of Halston III—he did not take the time to find out who she was and therefore what she actually wanted from her wardrobe. Middle America just did not like the Halston aesthetic, and the

---

buying public as they say: "stayed away in droves". Woe to him that patronizes his patron.

This is also when other aspects of "the deal" soured. Ownership of rights to Halston's name was flipped through a series of transactions during the mergers and acquisition happy early eighties, so that his eponymous aerie in the sky was finally owned outright by Beatrice foods, who proceeded to license the brand as they saw fit. (Hence, the apocryphal aquarium gravel from Walgreens.) Also, the corporation was not amenable to the deluxe excesses of Halston's day-to-day business operations. As ever, Halston epitomized glamour, and glamour does not come cheap. It could be argued though that he was a living breathing advertisement for his eponymous brand. 24-7 he was feted, surrounded by, and generally adulated by the cream of international high society. You can't buy publicity like that, the hundreds of thousands spent on orchids were actually a bargain. By the end however, he was having meals prepared at Olympic Tower and flown out on a private chartered plane to Montauk for picnics on the beach. Beatrice wasn't having it. As corporate structures re-oriented and evolved into the systems-driven strategies of the 80's, greater scrutiny was brought to all aspects of the chain. Beans were counted, and Halston was deemed an impossibly excessive expense. He had an undisturbed run of nine years of unparalleled lux though, before everything started to disintegrate.

A brand is a property that is purchased for a return on investment. It was still in the corporate interest to support Halston (one would think). This was not however the strategy employed by Beatrice. Instead, they went on the attack. Cue Tcheng's tedious managers spouting sports analogies and hollow justifications as to why they trashed the Halston mystique. One particularly egregious corporatist dullard recounts (with obvious relish) how he kept phoning Halston and sneering "we own your name", and by implication we own you. This obnoxious stooge took great pride in that he now had control of Halston's name, relating how he only called him "Roy" during their phone calls. "You don't own your name…" he taunts "…pal". His demeanour (for me anyway) had all the markings of the locker room bully who preys on smaller boys, brutally yanking their underwear up their ass crack for a "wedgie". Getting off on this and many other frat house-esque subjugations and humiliations of those weaker than themselves. It is not just women who are serially victimized and brutalized by the dominant within corporations. No, there is a certain type of man who is very generous with his cruelty, it makes for better control don't you know. It also appears to serve as a very enjoyable pastime for them. These attitudes are what some of the worst expressions of fraternal corporate culture is built upon. Illustrating the festering misanthropy that can often be found conjoined to their septic misogyny.

The sheer maliciousness heaped upon Halston was also reflected in the tag-sale dumping of the *entire* Halston archives for 25$ or 50$ a gown, which can only be seen as openly hostile and vindictive. Another imbecilic corporate flunky states that "It was just stuff sitting there year after year, doing nothing" (Tcheng 2019). When asked why it wasn't donated to an educational institution, unable to provide an answer, the

---

troglodyte just leaves the question hanging there, dead in the air. The philistines had stormed the citadel.

Pierre Cardin

It wasn't like Halston was the first to mass-market a name, Worth, Paquin and Poiret all sold licensed versions of their Parisian originals, and there are many (lovely) licensed Dior gowns held in prestigious collections internationally that are now featured in high profile museum exhibitions (including the Royal Ontario Museum in my hometown of Toronto). Yves Saint Laurent with *Rive Gauche* delivered an off-the-rack brand with more democratic connotations. However, with Rive Gauche, YSL still controlled the brand and the boutique; it was "accessible" only if you compared it to the rarified haute couture of the YSL atelier. Rive Gauche was ready to wear that was cheap*er* than the couture, it certainly wasn't *cheap*.

Figure 14 "Worth Gown" @Mark O'Connell
2021

The closest parallel to the Halston debacle was Pierre Cardin the Parisian designer and licensing king who made billions off his deals, and through this ensured his name will be forever linked to mountains of cheap umbrellas, ties fabricated from textiles of enigmatic material composition, acrylic everything, and the cheapest of cheap matching pen sets.

Cardin, however, as was recently illustrated by the excellent retrospective at the Brooklyn Museum was a very different breed of designer than our Halston. An examination of the Cardin oeuvre reveals that he was always designing a ready-to-wear, youthful, mass-market type of garment. His was as much an experiment in social consciousness as a fashion line. Akin to the glass and chrome environs of the Charles de Gaulle airport, Cardin clothes were made for the space-age new possibilities of his particular vision for a future-oriented France. Thus, the transition to mass market was easy for Cardin as he always designed for his own modernist utopia; a universalist cosmos of consumer engagement. Creative and cool geometric shapes, cut from Melton wool and stretch jersey in unisex styles, abound throughout the Brooklyn exhibition.

Ubiquity was one of his goals as he aspired to design for a new society en masse. Therefore, the roll out into panoplied, licensed production was uncomplicated by exclusivity. And while his cachet undoubtedly suffered as a result of the deluge of junk bearing his little curled logo, it wasn't like he was Balenciaga to start with. Plus, he laughed all the way to the bank, as he licenced with abandon but never sold his name outright, every new partnership was tied to new revenue, making him as rich as a czar, in fact he now owns the aforementioned Maxim's.

This was not Halston who was Park Avenue, with all those sumptuous triple weight cashmeres, that shiny silky and sequined simplicity. He attempted to bring this rarefied aesthetic to Main Street USA. And as anyone who has ever worked in fashion design knows, minimalist elegance and sartorial simplicity rely heavily on luxe constituent materials and a superlative quality of finish. Neither of which are options available for a mass market product.

Another point to consider is that inevitably styles change. Fashion is fundamentally nihilistic as the shock of the new relies on the demise of its recent predecessor. Halston was synchronous with the Mirabella era of Vogue. Where Diana Vreeland was supremely fantastic and over the top in her 1960's Vogue fashion fantasies, Grace Mirabella expertly mirrored the recessionary, high inflation, rapidly globalizing, but deliberately non-showy 70's. A Gucci loafer is very easy to walk in. Mirabella attempted to showcase a real woman—albeit one who still shopped at Sak's and Henri Bendel—who dropped her children off at daycare on her way to a career (as opposed to a volunteer or a social engagement). The Vogue woman was always beautiful and poised, but for Mirabella she possessed an agency in addition to the effortlessness of her elegant display. Mirabella's vision highlighted the hard-won gains of feminism as correlated to the new realities of increased autonomy and responsibility. However, as New York was rescued from the precipice of bankruptcy—and subsequently, once again better policed—an initially wary high society swan eventually re-emerged with a firm desire to leave the heavily recessed late seventies in her socio-cultural past.

With the advent of the Reagan boom boom boom years, the newly affluent—and those who had always been flush but were afraid of being mugged in the street if they flaunted it—now wanted to show off that wealth. They broadcasted it in baroque, showy, overtly luxurious, fundamentally expensive looking garments: "…'it's Lacroix darling'…'*fabulous*'". The Halston understated lux, and Grace Mirabella's modern working woman, were shoved out of the way by the triumphant new empresses of New York society and their $, **$, $**. Mirabella was unceremoniously dumped and replaced by Anna Wintour, and the unbridled adulation of gilded wealth that defined the eighties was unleashed. The corporate owners of the once-coveted, subsequently degraded Halston name (of course) continued to try and capitalize upon their asset. Over and over, faceless beanpickers attempted to revivify the mystique, with Sisyphean, soulless re-launches. These were tenuously tied to celebrity non-designers and unsurprisingly the tired, futile offerings quickly dissolved back into obscurity. The corporation had killed their goose that once laid the golden eggs.

"When I first Met Him": Shade on the Coffin

"There are no second acts in American lives"

F. Scott Fitzgerald, *The Last Tycoon* (1941)

As true today, as the day he died. The Halston legacy is now tarnished and possibly trashed past redemption. This is due in large part to his epitaphs. His obituaries had a consistent structure and "flavour". Initially laudatory, they quickly devolve into hectoring condemnation, variations of "Shame on you Halston, you had it all and you blew it". Like this malodorous one from *People* magazine from April 9th, 1990 (whose cover he graced in a photo wherein he is dutifully gazed upon by *both* Liza and Liz):

Halston 1932 – 1990; He put American fashion on the map; He dressed Jackie; Liz and Liza.

He died last

Week of AIDS

A broken man. (People 1990)

Inside, the magazine elaborated on their dissection of the corpse of their "broken man":

Suave and gracious, he was a kind of Jay Gatsby of Manhattan nightlife, a mysterious, aspiring Midwesterner who altered his name and re-created himself in a tanned and tuxedoed image of breathless glamour. It was Halston whose parties helped transform a cavernous Manhattan space called Studio 54 into the disco of the decade. It was Halston whose friendships with Liza and Liz gave a hot center to the celebrity culture and established him as the walker to the stars. And it was Halston whose simple designs in cashmere and Ultrasuede defined a newly self-confident American fashion sense. Gushed Women's Wear

Daily: "The 1970s belong to Halston." (Sporkin et. al 1990, pgh 2)

Yes, very impressive indeed, but you knew it wouldn't stop there...

> In late 1988 he found he was carrying the AIDS virus. The blows continued. Last year his former friend's revelations of drugs and debauchery in *The Andy Warhol Diaries* left him feeling embarrassed and betrayed. Like Gatsby, his dreams busted up before he did. (pgh 3)

And his eulogizers continue:

> Usually clad in a turtleneck or tux, he also attracted plenty of attention for his languid, polished mannerisms and un-apologetically dissolute life-style. The music had changed a little, and the barbarians now wore plaid double-knit jackets, but Nero would have felt right at home when Halston held court at Studio 54. (pgh 12)

Seriously?! The "languid" and "un-apologetically dissolute" holding court with Nero...this overripe description would be hilarious if it wasn't so laced with subtextual poisonous homophobic judgment and condemnation.

Yes, it could be argued that this is what Halston's life became, what the end of the seventies became. Halston was undoubtedly decadent and probably a bit gross by the end of the seventies, *but so was everybody else in his milieu*. Yet, his story is invariably presented as a singular morality tale. Homo Hubris; too gay, too flashy, too greedy, too addicted and *way* too out of control. AIDS could be the only conceivable end for him. The ending they obviously felt he deserved.

99

A fitting morality tale for that presumptuous, arriviste queen from Des Moines. And oh, how they laughed behind their crocodile tears in his eulogies. His obituaries read with a depressing ubiquity. Like this choice offering from "friend" Liz Smith:

> But there are no secrets, and Halston's downfall was inevitable. Unlike many of his friends, Halston never got himself to the Betty Ford Clinic or into rehabilitation. He died of AIDS in 1990. Everyone who knew Halston still mourns his loss, for he was a fashion original who had it all and threw it all away - not for a mess of biblical pottage, but for two or three or four thousand waterglasses full of cocaine. (Smith 1991, Pgh 6)

How poetic: "two or three or four thousand waterglasses full of cocaine", perhaps "Everyone who knew Halston still mourns his loss" but it doesn't seem to stop any of them from trashing him…ad infinitum. Also, was he doing all that coke alone? This all seems to come down to a particularly puritanical variety of fag-bashing, slut-shaming or pietistic condemnation.

Downfall of the Trained Faggot Poodles

> She picked up her mother's apple-green-bordered Meissen dinner plate that Hubie had used and looked at it, in a porcelain farewell. Then she dropped the plate on the

pantry floor and watched it smash into irretrievable disrepair. (215)

Dominick Dunne *People Like Us*, 1989

The word that keeps coming up in descriptions of Halston is "glamour", but there is another word that also has strong connotations when discussing the Halston persona. Apparently Halston was at a party in the Hamptons during the mid-sixties, and some establishment "gentlemen" stood behind their chairs after everyone else had been seated for dinner...they would not be seated at a table with a *faggot*. Halston's former associate relates exactly what was said: "If these two faggots are at table we won't be joining you for dinner." They would not sully themselves by even eating at the same table as a homosexual. Charming. Halston said of the Hamptons homophobia incident "You and I could never hope to be anything more than trained faggot poodles...To jump through the hoops of these rich people" (Tcheng 2019). He was there to entertain, and in order to stay he had to stomach the homophobic abuse.

This type of homophobic hatred would certainly not play out ten years later during the mid-seventies at the height of Halston's success, when all of high society was begging to be included in his luminous spotlight. Yet it was a stigma and ignorance that would fully reassert itself a further ten years on, during the Reagan & AIDS afflicted mid-eighties. A time when all Gay men would be reduced and vilified as AIDS pariahs.

Halston's was a legacy and a public personality that was entirely played out through the media for a straight audience. (What else was there to play to in the 70's?!) He was the caricature of the Gay male designer. Along with Gore Vidal and Truman Capote, Halston was a famous "faggot"; in fact, he was he was probably the faggiest faggot in the world. In the media, in popular culture, there he was front and centre, and here he was in everyone's home and on their television sets. He was even on *Love Boat* FFS. Extremely handsome, yet at the same time singularly unattractive. Always surrounded by those impossibly beautiful (paid) women, yet no one thought for a minute he was fucking any of them, like the Olympic Tower orchids, they were the most exquisite of props, and en ensemble they generated endless photo-ops.

Halston was his own Pierre Bergé and YSL embodied in one solitary person. Both creative and executive. I can't imagine the toll that would take on a person. It certainly didn't make him nice to be around. In fact, he could be awful:

> [V]ast success brought out his dictatorial side. He could be bullying and abusive, unable to see others as humans rather than props in the theatre of his life. As his empire began to crumble, he insisted that staff at his Olympic Tower headquarters wore only black, and in the footage he appears hysterically tense, the lonely leader of an impossibly severe cult. (Hilton 2019, pgh. 7)

However, as Halston's lawyer points out in the Tcheng documentary, the unmanageability and drug issues don't actually come out for any public discussion until the corporation was trying to punish Halston and *push him out*.

102

One wonders how much of Halston's trashed and tarnished legacy has been disseminated as a cautionary tale spun by corporate America. Don't bite the hand that feeds you...*bitch*.

I'm not denying or excusing Halston's drug problems or his nasty attitude. But that wasn't the whole story, and many famous people were (and are) truly awful. (I worked in fashion for twenty years, trust me on this.) Fashion labels crash and burn all the time, yet the Halston story—thirty years and counting—is still the hottest topic in this arena. There clearly is more to it than just the unpredictability of fashion and licensing. When Halston fell down off the pedestal the laughing hyenas circled in for the evisceration. The name-and-shame politics of homophobic media representation pilloried him. His downfall when it finally came was such big news because it was eagerly anticipated, relished...feasted upon.

Lil Altemus, chilly, old money Park Ave matriarch from *People Like Us* (1989) intentionally breaks an heirloom plate her son had been eating from earlier in the evening, the reason? That was the evening he told her he had AIDS and was dying. After he leaves her palatial apartment, she dispassionately disposes of the plate—along with flatware from her wedding silver that he also ate with, and the crystal wineglass he drank from—all unceremoniously dumped into the trash. AIDS-phobia was as much a part of Halston's public downfall as that singularly bad deal. Halston had the hubris of the faggot who not only was freely accorded a prime seat at the head table, but eventually had become the one to choose who would be allowed to eat there with him. How could people have once looked up to that "faggot" they wondered once it all came crashing down? Upon his descent he would be made to pay for his presumption and arrogance. He died a social pariah according to the narrative spun by media representation.

AIDS in the 80s was the ultimate stigma, and as a result the sick were marginalized, vilified, and discarded. Halston was torn down and reduced to a pathetic diseased caricature. People don't like failure, and a lot of people don't like Gays (then and now). Gays with an attitude? Watch out honey, you have a target on your back. Halston was deliberately diminished due to the circumstances surrounding him when he died; henceforth (and in perpetuity) he would always be that "faggot".

The antipathy I felt towards the person, entirely obscured what a brilliant designer he actually was, and this reaction was taught to me, by the consensus of mass media who zealously named and shamed. Halston's persona made me uncomfortable because his representation made me feel ashamed of what I *was*. Yes, he could be nasty and loud, so what? He was also an unapologetically Queer man who came from humble means and made billion-dollar deals for himself. He singlehandedly created a uniquely American high fashion style. As he said, he "...made Americans believe in American style". That is remarkable. Yet, his historical representation is overwhelmingly prurient and trashy, something that Liza Minelli admonishes one of the documentary filmmakers for doing. In response Sulder-Smith provides a video clip of a jittery late-career Halston, ubiquitous sunglasses still on, looking (and sounding) haggard and strung out; with a swollen coldsore on his upper lip. He deserved better.

Posthumous, finger pointing condemnation is tired and it has been done; in fact, it is *all* that has been done with Halston's story. Time for some deeper subtlety in the understanding of his legacy.

Legacies: Lost in Music

"Studio 54 had a giant, smiling man in the moon up above the dancers slowly shoveling a spoon of cocaine toward his nose, over and over" (270).

City Boy, My Life in New York During the 1960s and '70s.
Edmund White

As a former bar star and refugee of the early 90s club scene. I can tell you for a fact that disco never died. Not for one single minute. The languid film noire jazz employed by Tcheng was definitely not Halston; disco on the other hand, now that was! The exuberant trumpets in "Get Down Tonight" (1975) by KC and the Sunshine Band were a lot closer to Halston energy. Sulder-Smith's waka waka, retro porn, Shaft-esque soundtrack was in fact much closer to what was wonderful about Halston. Sulder-Smith even managed to get Nile Rodgers of Chic fame talking about the scene, and seventies disco life. It was an era where very different worlds were coming together, and it was happening on a dance floor. Halston partied up in Harlem with Joel Schumacher, they could *move.*

Imagine for a moment that you are hearing "Freak Out" for the first time, in the hottest club? Surrounded by your clique, and you are all literally the most gorgeous? Of course, everyone feels like they are the hottest when their "it" song comes on at 2 a.m. and you make a mad dash for a spot on the dance floor, but these folks actually *were* the epicenter of cool of their time. They were very, very, sexy. Can you imagine Christian Dior getting down on a sweaty firetrap dancefloor in some West Village dive? Preposterous. They all actually were out on the floor... at *54* no less, gives you chills thinking about it. My head would probably explode from the fabulousness of it. Halston was even name checked in *He's the Greatest Dancer* by Sister Sledge, one of the finest dance tracks ever recorded..."Oh what a joy" indeed.

Disco was musical, and it was also situated in a particular locus of freedom. It was a place where people of all races (Gay people and loose straight people mostly) took centre stage on those illuminated dancefloors. What is overlooked in the (now) accusatory condemnation of those decadent times is how much fun they all had, at least in the early days. The zeitgeist was conceived in the environs of the disco certainly—the mirrored surfaces, smoke and cocaine—but it was larger than that. For it was also about the dance itself, the beautiful emancipatory movement of the body. The seventies were a no-underwear, woozy blowjob in a trash strewn back alley behind the Ritz kinda era. An era when a lot of beautifully attired—unapologetically slutty—men and women got it on. Perhaps, it isn't valued now, but these forms of freedom were both exhilarating, emancipatory and also so necessary. A freedom and liberation that would later be eclipsed by the moralistic, conservative condemnation of pleasure itself.

Tribute for an Emperor

When you move past "Glamour" and "Faggot" there is third descriptor that is appropriate to use when discussing the legend that is Halston. This third word is one that Halston himself uses frequently in his commentaries and interviews, and that is *freedom*. In archival footage, Halston can be seen adjusting the drape of fabric on one of his models. He thoughtfully repositions her into a contraposto pose during the fitting, the fabric slips away, sheer against skin, revealing a leg, a scapula, and then obscures them again. It was all designed to be moving and migrating across the body. Slinky, sexy, physically alluring through motion. This all resulted in a feeling of "…being naked with your clothes on" (Hilton 2019, pgh. 1); how marvelous, I would love to know what that would feel like. He freed the body from the rigidity of over-constructed couture. He freed American women from the dictates of European designers, and his zeitgeist aligned with that of the social and sexual freedom of the seventies. At his best (and even during his most dissolute and debauched times he was consistently, extremely good), Halston was pure poetry in motion, and always, always true to his unique quintessence.

Also, one thing that comes through clearly in both docs, is that Halston was dearly loved by the people he was closest to. He was difficult, but he also could be protective, loving and nurturing. He was also vulnerable, as Pat Cleveland said of him:

> Every decade has its very severe punishments for being who you are. The whole thing of being a homosexual man and growing up in situations where you want to express yourself, but you can't — that was Halston's experience. He had this curiosity and vulnerability, and he wanted so much to be loved deeply (Cleveland qtd. in La Ferla & Trebay 2019, Pgh 26).

His close friends were therefore deeply hurt at the end when he withdrew himself away from both them and his life in New York.

As for the circumstances of his actual demise:

> The end came at 11:22 P.M. on March 26 in Room 670 at Pacific Presbyterian Medical Center in San Francisco. Halston, 57, succumbed to Kaposi's sarcoma, an AIDS-related cancer, after an 18-month struggle with the disease whose chilling toll has already devastated the fashion industry (see following story) (Sporkin et. al 1990, pgh 4).

His premature death came after spending his final two years living with his family in San Francisco, having entirely retreated from life on the East Coast. He had nothing at all to do with his eponymous brand at that time yet was still receiving fat cheques from the corporation every single month. He may have been sick with full-blown AIDS, infuriated with that selfsame corporation, and actively working to get his name back, but he was also simultaneously driving around in the pure California sunshine in his Rolls Royce along the Pacific Coast highway. All the while making the calls he needed to make to try and orchestrate his resurrection. They never talked about that part of the deal in those awful, awful obituaries; for all the drama, until his last breath Halston got *paid*. There is no doubt in my mind that if Halston had lived long enough to benefit from the advances in AIDS medications there would have been a second act that would have been mind-blowing. In any case, he was anything but a "broken" man. Yes, he died hard, but his story should be retold as one of amazing achievements.

There is also a marked repudiation of the notion of sensuality in the treatment of Halston's legacy. A state of being which is held suspect in our moralizing, deeply conservative, post-AIDS times. It is a fundamentally puritanical, admonitory, and also very boring attitude, everything Halston was definitely not. What the posthumous narrative boils down to is an embarrassed apologia as to how could a culture have been that unapologetically sybaritic, how could we have given ourselves up so wholeheartedly to something so simple and satisfying, the sweetest taboo: *pleasure.*

Ultimately, it is unjust to judge a thirty-year career—one that was for the most part punctuated only with unprecedented successes and innovation—solely by the inarguably disappointing final five years. (However ghastly the latter may have appeared at times.) When you look at the work, the entire Halston oeuvre, it is clear he deserves a better eulogy. Doing a promo video for JC Penney in 1983, when asked how he wished to be remembered in fashion history he replied with: "maybe we cleaned it up a bit, I have a theory that less becomes more." (Halston qtd. in VideoFashion 2009). This is not unfortunately how he is remembered; yet no one designed understated, wearable American elegance better than Halston. To feel freed and so lightly attired as to approach the sensation of nakedness while moving your body on the dance floor, how divine. To feel simultaneously comfortable, sensual and supremely stylish, what could be more luxurious than that?

Reflections on Stigma

I have a friend, a personal trainer, who was at the gym in downtown Toronto where we are both members. In the showers one young queen remarked to another (about my friend): "that is what the body of someone with long-term AIDS looks like", easily within his earshot. The utter callous cruelty of that statement appalled me. And I felt so angry on behalf of my friend, who is a survivor, who saw everyone around him cut down by AIDS, most of his friends, acquaintances, the whole first generation of the Gay liberation movement in Toronto; All are gone now.

Throughout this, he kept his strength up, maintained his body, maintained his equilibrium, maintained his *sanity*! Weathering these slings and arrows of outrageous misfortune. He survived and he tried the best he could, and he triumphed. He fought back against the disease, he underwent all of the corrosive early treatments and medication, he felt the multitude of painful side-effects of these cocktails that were saving his life even as they took their toll on his physical body. he saw his face so changed that it resembled the "cigar store Indian", as described by

Armistead Maupin (Maupin 2008, 15). Plastic surgery eventually evolved to the point where it was able to return the contours of his face back to the days of pre-AZT. But there has not been an open-heart surgery developed that can restore the pain of his massive agglomerate losses.

He is an intelligent, opinionated and very strong-willed man to this day, so to be so casually dismissed, and described in such an ugly, damaging way. No. He deserves better. His take on the incident? He said offhandedly: "It's true, this *is* what a body with long term AIDS looks like". My friend's body is beautiful, he's muscular, he's well shaped, he is very desirable. He was far more magnanimous than I felt he needed to be; I was ready to go after those callus and cruel little monsters with a baseball bat.

All very *Gay*.

Chapter Three: "Way Bandy: Kiss and Make Up"

Lipstick

I have a tale to tell

Sometimes it gets so hard to hide it well

I was not ready for the fall

Too blind to see the writing on the wall

Madonna "Live to Tell" *True Blue*, 1986

A figure crouches in the middle of an immense, darkened room. She pokes her head up, almost like an animal from a burrow, looking out for danger, examining the terrain. She's lit by very bright spotlights, they single her out and isolate her. In the dark around her there are figures lurking, difficult to discern in the shadows. Akin to the dancers performing as wilis from Giselle, they exist in a choreographed half-light darkness. One of them addresses her directly: "You look so beautiful today…it's nice like that, just turn your head away a little bit, turn it away…bring it back to me…so beautiful …c'mon you're my favourite girl…You're my favourite girl in the whole world". It is Francesco Scavullo, and he is photographing this woman. Photographing her face. Up close, she is radiant and lovely. Although heavily made up for this commercial beauty photo shoot there is a naturalness to the maquillage. Very light freckling across her forehead is discernible through the foundation, her eye shadow has a rich topaz hue, all blended so smoothly—a renaissance chiaroscuro— a dusky corona for her extraordinary aqua eyes. Eyelashes curl away to better reveal those amazing eyes, those windows to the soul. Brows are lightly shaped upward and away, opening up the upper half of her face. A peach blusher is brushed high on her already naturally elevated cheekbones, but like the hollows on her face and her contouring, it is all done in shades analogous to her natural skin tones. A high gloss reflects from her very full mouth, but the stain is again, close to her natural skin tone, and there is no hard, defining lip line penciled in. As mentioned, a full face of heavy makeup has been applied to her skin, but somehow it still looks fresh and entirely natural. Her planar spectacular face, with her wide-open expression: equal parts sculptural supermodel bones, and unguarded expressiveness is utterly captivating. Until the lower lip begins to tremble, the expression devolves from ethereal madonna to fear and despair. Her entire persona crumbles, she turns away from the light, rises from her crouch and retreats into a darkened corner of the studio

"Kill it Bob" snaps the photographer: Scavullo.

Hers is a signature beauty, a famous face from an even more famous lineage, she is Margaux, named after the wine her parents drank on the night of her conception, she is the granddaughter of Ernest Hemingway. Margaux, one of the most famous models from the 70's, and the fragility exhibited on film was an expression of an inherent personal vulnerability as hers was not an easy life. One of those beautiful souls who lack a protective layer, she would fight mental health and addiction issues all through her life (Holloway 1996). And like many a vulnerable diva before her, appreciated the support of her Gay friends.

The scene is from *Lipstick* (1976) a not-great film, with some really great fashion content. For this film there was only one makeup artist who was allowed to work on the face of the female lead (Rowes 1978). The particularities of the maquillage are all signature techniques pioneered by him. He is also *in* the film, one of the wraiths in this scene. All in black, lissome, Way Bandy stands up and walks (glides) away on tip toe away as the photographer tries to comfort the disheartened young woman. Bandy, was more than just a successful artist (Although successful he certainly was, the number one makeup artist in the world for much of his career, he pioneered the role of the makeup artist-as-guru.) No, he was also an advocate for a much more expansive notion of beauty: a sacred holism of practical regime and life. He also looked out for his models, bringing a compassion and care to his work on the most famous faces in the world. Fabulous Gays and divas…you can't have one without the other.

*Figure 16 "Margaux Hemingway from Lipstick,
Makeup: Way Bandy" @Mark O'Connell 2021*

Lost in Music

The 1960's and 1970's were vital eras of social expansion and heightened emancipation for Gay men.

Within the subcultural ghettos of Toronto, San Francisco, New York, London, Paris, Los Angeles, Sydney, Montreal, Milan, there was a new opportunity and freedom afforded to Gay men that had never been available before. They ran with it. The world of fashion and design benefitted enormously from their ascendent, exuberant expression. Fashion design, acquisition and display are clear communicators of zeitgeist. Pierre Bourdieu in *Distinction a Social Critique of the Judgement of Taste* (1979) explored how objects as lifestyle signifiers are coveted as a way of communicating a superior social position, and a way of acquiring "cultural capital". However, not everyone is motivated by a desire to communicate their upward mobility.

In the 1970's young people were getting loose with liberation; their cultural capital was of a very hedonistic variety and they clearly communicated this through the fashions of the times. Satin shirts open to the waist for men, one shouldered draped chiffons for women, everything silky, sliding over the body, in turns revealing then concealing. The communication of disco era divas and studs was unmistakable, they were out for *fun*, in and out of their streamlined, body conscious attire. They visually broadcast the question Rod Stewart raunchily rasped out in the 1978 hit "Do ya think I'm sexy?" Epitomized by such fashion-world beauties as Margaux Hemingway, the 70's aesthetic expressed a highly sexualized naturalness. The body was the focus, physical expression was through dance, the venue was the nightclub, and everybody had a pretty amazing time until last call.

Fashion is an expression of the cultural mythologies that dominate an era, I would include the creation and presentation of the contemporaneous face within this mythmaking. The beauty iconography created by Bandy is an important cultural record as it was so imbricated within the larger glamour tropes of the 70's, and the draped, dancing luxury of disco divahood. Bandy's visual aesthetic perfectly reflected an era whose scintillating, liquid silhouettes, glistening lips and alluring beckoning eyes echoed the promises of liberatory ease and an empowered sexuality for anyone who dared. Unlike the Bar Suit by Dior that was so architectural and structured that it nearly stood up by itself; for disco era sirens, you really just needed to toss one of these floaty gowns on, add a strappy evening sandal, an Elsa Peretti cuff, and you were off to the dancefloor to get lost in music. If this chapter had a soundtrack I would be blasting Sister Sledge, Donna Summer, Sylvester, and of course Chic! Please feel free to listen along to funky disco at home.

Way Bandy

That's some starlet's nose on Way Bandy. he acquired it in '71 from a marvelous plastic surgeon recommended by one of the women who pay him $2,000 a shot to dip his long, mime's fingers into jars and paint cheekbones on them. To create the porcelain Way Bandy look that shows up on models on the covers of Cosmopolitan, Vogue, television commercials, even on Elizabeth Taylor. (9)

The Gadsden Times, 1979

It is early August 1986, New York City, Way Bandy had been scheduled for a shoot with Francesco Scavullo at the latter's famous coach house studio on East 69th. He arrived delirious and too exhausted to work. Described as a "tall, slender, pretty man in black shirt, black trousers, gray sweater and red scarf" (*The Gadsden Times* 1979, 9), and someone who would be bent by a breeze (Cunningham 1976) this was the day the bough could bear no more weight and collapsed. Up until this time Bandy had been relying on alternative medical treatments of his own design. By now his beautiful linen suits were hanging more and more loosely off his now too-lean frame (Polman 1986). His deep mistrust of doctors made it difficult for friends to effectively address his persistent fits of coughing that summer. He was not listening; he was determined to heal himself.

Way Bandy apparently spoke with a "Molasses drawl", and honey, he was nobody's fool. He kept his makeup in British antique silver bottles (Cunningham 1976, 127). Sometimes he poured commercial makeup in his little jars, sometimes he prepared his own concoctions as he recalled with amusement: "Just so the hairdresser doesn't know what's in them. A lot of people think if they can do hair, they can do makeup." (Bandy qtd. in Cunningham 1976, 127). They could not, not like Bandy. He cleansed the faces he worked on with avocado and olive oils, advocating natural cleanses, organic treatments.

To me, as I study him in a Scavullo photograph wherein he applies makeup to the face of a model, he looks like the love child of Alain Delon and Gloria Vanderbilt.

He was born Ronald Duane Wright in Birmingham, Alabama (*The Gadsden Times* 1979), but you would not know that if you became acquainted with him post 1970. After that time, he broke forever from his past and was definitively: "Way", a "wraith slim" sylphlike beauty oracle of unknown provenance. And there was a *lot* of baggage he dumped along with Ronald Duane.

According to Bandy, as a child he always had a "great interest in things female" as opposed to "traditional masculine things—fishing, hunting, baseball" (Rowes 1978, 9). He grew up in an environment where "All his family were with the railroad". He categorized himself as an:

> [A]nachronism. My parents and I had different ideas about everything. What I ate, the shoes I wore, and I had two brothers who were absolutely normal [...] when we suffer these hurts and misunderstandings in childhood, we want to carve a life that's comfortable for our understanding of things (Rowes 1978, 9).

There was however room for expression on a canvas, even in that limited environment. His father drew the line at ballet though, another passion of the young Bandy. There would be no performing Hilarion—or Giselle for that matter (Bandy actually resembled the latter more)—for the young Way.

While his father was definitely not supportive of his *feminized* interests, there was also a mother in that house, and she did:

> From the earliest moment I can remember...I was different. A strange member of a traditional middle-class family. My mother taught me how to sew, gave me piano

lessons and even bought me baby dolls (Bandy qtd. in Rowes 1978, 9).

[Thank heaven for sympathetic mothers, in my case both my parents indulged my obdurate, and at times intractable desire for Barbies, but it was *verboten* for my beauties to leave the house.] Bandy's mother also had a friend who slipped him movie magazines. From these, he painted portraits of the glittering stars. Redoing their makeup as he saw fit: "He loved the glamorous faces— Betty Grable, Elizabeth Taylor, Marilyn Monroe" (Rowes 1978, 8). The likenesses were not entirely literal however: "I would make them up the way I thought they should look...That's how I learned about cosmetics—it's a direct outgrowth of my painting." (Bandy qtd. in Rowes 1978, 10). It wasn't just the faces of the famous beauties he was experimenting on. Bandy was fascinated with looking different even as a young child, the transformative power of makeup, trying it out on his own face:

> I can remember when I was about eight looking in the bathroom mirror and thinking if I had a little sheen on my cheeks they'd look better. I took my father's hair oil and rubbed it on to make them shiny. This was to go to church. Can you imagine? (Bandy qtd. in Lavin 1981, 2B)

I can imagine. Brave little boy, finding his own way in a world that was definitely not made for him:

> I wasn't interested in baseball and football like my two brothers. I liked reading and painting. Everyone else was made to take piano lessons. I wanted to ...Now as an adult, I cultivate different people. I celebrate individuality. I respond to it. I often think that wouldn't it be terrific if

everyone tried to look different instead of alike? (Bandy qtd. in Lavin 1981, 2B)

Yes, it really would be terrific!

One-time painted portrait subject Elizabeth Taylor (later a client) stated of Bandy: "He works like an artist. He mixes colors in the palm of his hand like a painter with a palette" (Taylor qtd. in Rowes 1978, 8). The fine art techniques gained from painting, later, informed his superlative makeup application. He was often connected to fine art traditions in descriptions of his work, and interestingly also of his person: El Greco, Giacometti (Trebbe 1986); all slender elongation. He was his own masterpiece.

High school saw him voted the "best dressed, most talented and biggest flirt." He was a member of a fraternity at Birmingham-Southern College, and apparently "...always the last to leave a party". He then dropped out of school to become a department store model. Later completing a degree in English from the Tennessee Technological University, after which he embarked on a career as an educator: "We have many pressures and fears in youth and I suppose I was afraid to make that leap and make art my life work, and I did enjoy English." (Bandy qtd. in Lavin 1981, 2B). Bandy taught high school English for four years.

He also married.

Then, in the summer of 1965, Bandy and his spouse took a trip to NYC and as he later described it: "The minute we arrived I knew I would never go back to my former life. This was a new beginning." (Bandy qtd. in Rowes 1978, 12). They separated (never divorced), he moved to NYC, jettisoned Ronald Duane Wright and never looked back.

Bandy went through a radical personal reinvention during this time. He had his teeth were capped, nose done, and face lifted with a "temporal lift (with the incision in his hairline)" (Rowes 1978, 8). He was what, twentysomething at the time? No one knew for sure because he was so notoriously secretive (Polman 1986). He also rechristened himself Way Bandy. He said the "The name just came into my consciousness" (Polman 1986). Actually, it was a name he lifted from a boy he knew back in Alabama.

Upon arrival in Manhattan in 1966, Bandy attended the Christine Valmy Beauty School, where he learned his technical skills of make-up application as well as the larger skills of skin preparation, and aesthetics. He quickly capitalized on his teaching experience and became a faculty member of the school, as well as the "dermaspecialist". This focus on healthy skin and the foundational aspects of make-up was to be a constant all through his career.

Bandy than became makeup director of Charles of the Ritz, legendary purveyor of superlative cosmetic, fragrance, and esthetic experiences. Located at E57th and Park Avenue, the Charles of the Ritz beauty salon was described as a "forever-springtime world of sunshine and lightness...an atmosphere of never-ending beauty" the new salon was described as a "pleasant mix of opulence and modern practicality" and one "highlighted" by a sculptural "assemblage" by Gloria Vanderbilt, a "fascinating work of art designed especially for the salon". This consisted of a "charmingly nostalgic four-dimensional collection of beauty memorabilia [which] greets you on entering and with wit and subtlety denotes the transition of beauty through the ages" (Gogick 1972, 14) one wonders about the fourth dimension, was the installation fragrant?

Although largely forgotten today, Charles of the Ritz was a hugely successful cosmetics and fragrance company that grew out of a salon situated in the Ritz Carlton. The Jean Naté line and the skincare and makeup divisions of the Yves Saint Laurent Beauté brand were both Charles of the Ritz initiatives (the latter brand was actually owned by Charles of the Ritz from 1963 to 1986); as well as the following fragrances:

Jean Naté 1935; Spur 1937; Tingle 1938; Summertime 1939; Wintertime 1940; Love Potion 1941; Spring Rain 1941; Flower Show 1942; Jester 1944; Sea Shell 1944; Soignee 1944; Water Sprite 1944; An English Garden 1945; Damask 1945; Little Women 1945; Ritual 1945; Baby Pink 1947; Directoire 1948; French Provincial 1949; Floreal 1950; Country Wedding 1951; Charles of the Ritz 1977; Enjoli 1978; Charivari 1978; Forever Krystle 1984; Carrington 1984; Xi'a Xi'ang 1987. (cosmetics and skin.com)

These exclusive, pampering and rejuvenatory environs were where he initially met fashion photographer Scavullo. Theirs would prove to be a highly fruitful creative partnership. *WWD* quickly christened Bandy "Deee-vine" and since his discovery, he "floated through a cloud of Joy" (127). The fragrance one would imagine, but it is a nice thought to be floating through life clouded in the emotion of joy....

Bandy left the Ritz to become the principal artist for *No, No, Nanette* on Broadway in 1971 (Fried 1994, 122). [As one does.] After the closing of the show, he went out on his own as a freelancer, collaborating with such luminaries as Irving Penn, Richard Avedon, Skrebneski, Hiro, Horst P. Horst, and Helmut Newton; and working on shoots for Vogue, Cosmopolitan, Harper's Bazaar and Rolling Stone (NYT 1986); and *always* Scavullo.

Bandy became the most sought-after makeup artist in the world:

> He gets to make Brooke Shields look older. He gets to make everyone else look younger. and every five years or so he writes a book on how he does it all, and then he goes out into the heartland of America and sells it (Lavin 1981, 2B).

That brazen *Cosmopolitan* cover girl with her hybrid macho-sexy glamazonian magic? You can thank Way Bandy in part for her.

Capitalizing on his skills allowed him to create a hugely successful career and life for himself, he essentially created the role of the modern makeup artist while he was plying his trade:

> I was really a pioneer in this kind of thing which I started when I worked for Christine as a resident dermaspecialist. My interest was growing in makeup all the time and I started teaching makeup at her salon, step by step application. There was no such thing in New York then. Models did their own makeup for commercials and print

ads period so by teaching that class and working in a salon I really perfected the concept and technique of makeup application (Gadsden Times 1979, 9).

He worked on the most beautiful and famous faces in the world:

Cher, Barbara Walters, Elizabeth Taylor, Cheryl Tiegs, Lee Radziwill, Catherine Deneuve and Helen Gurley Brown all put their faces into his hands before important photo sessions. He has even had fleeting interludes in the makeup room with Mick Jagger, Mikhail Baryshnikov, Kris Kristofferson and Peter Frampton (Rowes 1978).

[Sorry, I'm unsuccessfully trying to keep my mind off of a fleeting interlude with Mikhail Baryshnikov...where were we?] According to a 1976 issue of *Cosmopolitan*: "He can make anyone prettier. He can also make anyone *poor...*" (Cunningham 1976, 127). He could "...turn skin into satin. Carve beauty out of mere flesh. Create a hollow, a shadow, a curve." (Lavin 1981, 2B). His lifelong love of painting found other outlets as Bandy did all the illustrations for his books *Designing Your Face* (1977) and *Styling Your Face* (1982). The visibility and celebrity resulted in great financial success. As a result, he had homes in Key West, Nantucket and Manhattan.

Described as a "kind and private" man (Trebbe 1986, 24), he enjoyed his great success:

"One of my favorite, favorite memories," said Hopson of the Nantucket days, "was sitting in a grassy knoll with a pond in front and then the dunes and then the ocean and eating lima bean sandwiches. There were lima beans, scallions, homemade mayonnaise and homemade bread. And we sat in silence looking at the pond. It was like an Andrew Wyeth painting. Those are the kind of moments you had with him. The famous women had those kinds of times with him, too" (Hopson qtd. in Trebbe, 24).

Bandy was also protective of the models he worked with, which is unfortunately not always the case in the fashion industry. He felt that the extreme youth of models was problematic:

> I do not select the models... The advertising agency or the magazine editor does that. I'm just employed to apply – cosmetics. When I'm working, a face is just a face to me. I don't think about the girls age. Being that young is really not that great an advantage (Bandy qtd. in Lavin 1981, 2B).

Going on to suggest that the use of extremely young models was as a result of laziness. That it took more work to beautifully photograph someone older: "I think this trend to very young models just comes out of boredom." (Bandy qtd. in Lavin 1981, 2B). He made the extra effort and was rightly known for appreciating and highlighting what was very beautiful in older women. This no doubt attributed to his huge commercial success; children do not book top-tier makeup artists.

He also contested the apocryphal narratives of "top models arriving for work drugged, dirty, unprepared to face the cameras" (Lavin 1981, 2B). To that last point I concur. I would also counter the aspersions that models are unintelligent. They are not, they are just very, very, young. A 13-year-old is a 13-year-old, even if she's made up to look like Aphrodite, she is still just a child. It was always amazing to me the transformative power of a good hair and makeup team. The young women who would be cast in a fashion show I was working on would

127

arrive early in the morning at the appointed call time, bleary eyed, coffees in hand, laughing and gossiping, blinking away sleep. Just a gaggle of tall lanky schoolgirls, long thin limbs; supremely casual. Choreography and rehearsals would follow, and then they were sent off to hair and makeup. Then came the alchemy, WOW! Magically, a battalion of unbelievably beautiful and glamorous sirens would return to take their places in the show lineup. I honestly wouldn't recognize many of them.

Feeding your Face

Zucchini is soaking in his Manhattan sink. His Acme Juicerator is pulverizing the carrots. Nine different vitamin pills are lying out on the counter. At 10:30 on a Saturday night, Way Bandy, zealous vegetarian and the world's leading makeup artist, is preparing the week's diet of organic food for soaking in Clorox—one half teaspoon in a gallon of water. "The Clorox raises its energy level and removes insecticides" Way believes (Rowes 1978).

Speaking of models and makeup, and in particular Bandy-specific tips and techniques; he said of all these personal innovations: "they're my hook." Not a hook to trick or ensnare for nefarious purposes though. No, Bandy believed he had a higher calling, as he said:

I think maybe it's part of my purpose in life to make people aware through cosmetics of how important nutrition is. Anything we put on or in our body has a chemical or electromagnetic influence on our skin. That's what we have to alert people to (Bandy qtd. in Gadsden Times 1979, 9).

His preoccupation with healthy living originated in a health crisis he experienced around 1960 when he was...well who knows how old he was, he was in college anyway. Bandy almost died from pneumonia and pleurisy, He survived and became a lifelong advocate of alternative healing modalities. He attributed this breakdown of health to an unhealthy lifestyle: "I used to smoke and do terrible things. It finally got through that nutrition is one way to control our body and therefore our life, so I started reading and learning about it." He advocated naturopathy, vitamin therapy, iridology (study of the Iris for health indicators), iniseology ("touch and vibration" therapy) colon irrigation: "when the walls of the intestines are clean, assimilation of the food can occur", weeklong fasting. He also advocated foot baths (Gadsden Times 1979, 9). Primarily it was all about the food though:

> "Nutrition is the key to beautiful skin, and that comes first. So you don't have to cover – you can decorate with makeup." His own skin gleams porelessly, unpolluted by fried foods (carcinogenic!) or toxic combinations "Forget eating starch with protein: eat one thing at a time – the mixture is what causes all the *putrefication*" (Cunningham 1976, 127).

He came up with his own strategies, regimens and systems of cleansing of his food:

> ...I found a way to get all the poison out of my food... And I don't have to buy everything organic. It sounds bizarre but I soak everything I eat in a Clorox solution: one capful Clorox to a gallon of tap water. I soak a thick skin fruit,

like a grapefruit, for 15 minutes. Thin skin, such as a grape, for 10. The Clorox takes out all the metallics... You know potatoes have arsenic in their skins before you soak them? Anyway, soaking raises the energy level of vegetables (Cunningham 1976, 128).

He also employed unorthodox methods of measuring the vitality in his food:

> I measure all my food with the pendulum and protractor period you insert the protractor in the fruit – measure the arc of the pendulum – maximum is 360 (127-128) degrees. A lot of food is practically dead when it comes from the market. I've gotten some very low readings – 80 for an apple – before soaking. After soaking, the energy count shoots up. So I always soak and measure. Why eat a dead potato if you can avoid it? (Cunningham 1976, 128).

Why would you eat a dead potato if it could be avoided? Described as someone who "survives on less food than it would take to keep a hummingbird on the wing" (Cunningham 1976, 127). He assiduously followed a meatless, non-fried health regime: "I am...perhaps as pure a fruitarian – vegetarian as you'll find in this city." (Bandy qtd. in 127); indeed. This healthiness and attention to the healing potential of food would all too soon become a desperate imperative.

The first wave of AIDS by necessity catalyzed a new philosophy of mind-body awareness. The faith healing, the obsession with pure and healthy eating, the fanatical removal of "impurities", all moved to the forefront of self-care when the tidal wave hit.

Stratagems for self-care adopted by terrified desperate men. There were no medications at that time. Also, cosmetics and self-care have been conjoined since the earliest days. Bandy's was a healing paradigm deeply rooted in the history of his artform.

Adwiyat al-Zinah: The Medicine of Beauty

A cardinal, that highte Saint Jerome,

That made a book against Jovinian,

Which book was there; and eke Tertullian, Chrysippus,
Trotula, and Heloise,

That was an abbess not far from Paris;

And eke the Parables of Solomon,

Ovide's Art, and bourdes many one;

And alle these were bound in one volume. (476)

Geoffrey Chaucer. "Wife of Bath" *The Canterbury Tales,
and Other Poems* ([1387 to 1400] 2012)

The etymology of the actual word 'cosmetics' comes from a Roman term *cosmetae* which denoted a slave whose primary service was the bathing of men and women in perfume (Eldridge 2015, 30); while the modern definition of cosmetics, according to the US food and drug administration, covers anything that is 'rubbed, poured, sprinkled, or sprayed on, introduced into, or otherwise applied to the human body... For cleansing, beautifying, promoting attractiveness, or altering the appearance' (15). Around the world, the use of cosmetics has a long tradition and the desire to adorn the body may predate the adoption of clothing itself (Wilson 2003). According to Lisa Eldridge in *Face Paint, the Story of Makeup* (2015) from the earliest times of human existence the painting of the body and the face served as 'a form of protection from the elements [...] as camouflage' (15), as well as served ritualistic purposes:

> Large quantities of red ocher (a pigment that takes its reddish color from the mineral hematite) discovered in excavations of South African caves are estimated to date back 100 to 125,000 years ago. The fact that there are no cave paintings or decorated artifacts at these sites has led archaeologists to believe that the ochre was used to paint the face and body (Eldridge 2015, 15).

Eldridge identifies this as a form of 'prehistoric cosmetics' and she identifies how ingredients like 'chalk, manganese dioxide, carbon, lapis lazuli, copper ore, and red and yellow ocher' were used to 'adorn and embellish in every corner of the globe'. These embellishments range from '...aboriginals and tribes of Papua New Guinea' on through to the 'earliest civilizations of Mesopotamia in Egypt' (Eldridge 2015, 17). From as early as 10,000 BC both women and men anointed themselves with fragrant oils and used balms to soften and cleanse skin, as well as minimize body odour. Creams, unguents and oils were used for 'protection against the hot Egyptian sun and dry winds'. Henna was employed to stain nails, lips were rouged along with cheeks with a red ochre coloured clay. Kohl derived from 'crushed antimony, burnt almonds, lead, oxidized copper, ochre, ash, malachite, chrysocolla (a bluegreen copper ore) or any combination thereof' (90) was applied with a small stick around the eyes to extend the eyes, and was used both for cosmetic purposes to create an almond shape, as well as to reduce the glare from the sun, it was also believed that kohl eyeliner 'protected the eyes from infection and strong sunlight' (17). For the ritual embalming of the dead 'Myrrh, thyme, marjoram, chamomile, lavender, lily, peppermint, rosemary, cedar, rose, aloe, olive oil, sesame oil and almond oil' (Jain & Chaudhri 2009, 164) were all utilized. The use ritualized application of topical ornamentation or tattooing can be found in many cultures. Warriors in preparation for battle often applied markings to call down the favour of the Gods (Hambly ([1920] 2009). In Japan powdered rice was used to lighten the face and back, and crushed safflower petals were applied as lipcolours, as well as to paint the edges of the eyes). Kohl (also called kajal) has a long history in South Asian cultures (Jain & Chaudhri 2009, 166). Eldridge notes that the Ancient Egyptians brought a particular sophistication to their maquillage:

> The ancient Egyptians are mainly remembered (in beauty circles) for their incredible eye makeup, but they were also renowned for their bold use of red, painting their lips of the vivid, early form of lipstick made by blending fat with red ocher period cheek rouge, also made from the same ingredients and possibly blended with wax or resin, gave cheeks a lacquered red luster that would have been garishly offset by emerald green eyelids and licorice black coal rimmed eyes (Eldridge 2015, 24).

Historically, cosmetics were not only deployed to enhance personal attractiveness. War paint was also used to denote and strengthen tribal allegiances in many First Nations populations (Redmond 1994; Matthews 1971). The ancient Britons for example, who painted their faces blue with dye produced from the leaves of the woad plant before going into battle (Eldridge 2015, 15). Anyone who has seen Braveheart will certainly remember those vivid blue faces plunging into battle.

The healing potentialities of cosmetics and procedures have also long been codified and included in treatises (medical and otherwise). The Roman poet Ovide, Publius Ovidius Naso (43 bc–17 AD) authored a treatise on cosmetology published circa five BC: *Medicamina Faciei Foeminarum*, which was also known as 'The Art of Beauty', of this there are one hundred lines surviving. Ovide adopted a poetic exploration of his subject and his was a not a scientific approach per se. Gaius Plinius Secundus, also known as Pliny the Elder, Roman 'physician, pharmacologist and botanist' (c. 40 ad–c. 90 ad) was the author of *Naturalis Historia, Pedanius Dioscorides* (Cavallo et. al 2008, 82). An encyclopedic study that spans thirty-seven books which examined his contemporaneous culture and society, and one that covered as well the 'medicinal uses of plants and animals' (Murphy 2004, 30), these included 'agriculture, horticulture and materia medica' in volumes xxviii through xxxii (Sandys 1911, n.p.). It is ironic, however, that Pliny is thought to have died at fifty-six of a heart attack during an attempt to rescue the Senator Pomponianus from the erupting volcano Vesuvius at Pompeii: as a result of his own corpulence:

A medical man may be excused for believing that Pliny died from apoplexy following unusual exertion and excitement, or possibly from a fatal crisis in some disease of the heart previously existing (Bigelow 1859, 227).

The physician Abu'al-Qassim al-Zahrawil, or Abulcassis (936-1013 AD), was an early proponent of cosmetology. al-Zahrawil authored a medical encyclopedia that spanned thirty volumes, it was number nineteen that was 'devoted to cosmetics'. Al- Zahrawi included cosmetics- which he called Medicine of Beauty: *Adwiyat al-Zinah*- as a branch of medicine, which he called Medicine of Beauty (Adwiyat al-Zinah). His work described the formulation and application of 'perfumes, scented aromatics and incense', as well as 'perfumed stocks rolled and pressed in special moulds'; the latter, some of the earliest examples of lipsticks and 'solid deodorants' (Jain & Chaudhri 2009, 165). This treatise was subsequently translated into Latin, and the information was made available outside of the Middle East.

There was also the early medieval *Schola Medica Salernitana* which originated in Salerno Italy, which was considered 'the most important native source of medical knowledge in Europe at the time'. The school came to prominence between the tenth and thirteenth centuries. The legend of the foundation of the school around 900 AD was the result of the meeting of 'four masters', and these were the: 'Jewish Helinus, the Greek Pontus, the Arab Adela and the Latin Salernus'. This synthesis of diverse wisdom saw the continuance of the 'Greek–Latin cultural tradition' but saw it 'merge harmoniously' with Jewish and Arab knowledge traditions (Cavallo et al 2008, 80). Contributions attributed to the *Schola Medica*

Salernitana were as follows: the creation of anatomy textbooks, the 'insistence on certification and training for physicians', encouragement of the 'application of investigative thinking and deduction', and this in turn 'led to important advances such as the use of healing by secondary intention [and] the first textbook about aesthetics medicine'. The scholarship from the Schola Medica Salernitana 'crossed borders' as Salernitan manuscripts were kept in 'many European libraries' and historical references. The location of the school in proximity to the 'most ancient' of the European botanical gardens located on a 'hillock on the seaboard of the town' (Cavallo et al 2008, 80): The Gardens of Minerva, where medicinal plants were grown and used to treat numerous illnesses.

A progressive place, the *Salernitana* included female physicians and students within their institution. They also had the 'first recorded female medical school member': one Trotula de Ruggiero, who was referred to as 'Magistra Mulier Sapiens (The wise woman teacher)'. de Ruggiero contributed to a textbook *Passionibus Mulierium Curandarum* first published c. 1100 AD that 'gained wide acceptance and distribution throughout Europe'. In fact, more than one hundred versions of the manuscript were found in Western Europe. It was a prominent text until a subsequent, significant revision by Ambrose Paré's assistant during the early 1600s. Paré was the 'pre-eminent anatomist of his time, and many of his important anatomic and surgical considerations were directly and indirectly derived' from the scholarship of de Ruggiero.

Trotula de Ruggiero eventually achieved such a high profile in the Middle Ages that her name can be found in *The Canterbury Tales* by Chaucer (1388–1400). The work of de Ruggiero that is most interesting however, is her study of ameliorative cosmetic procedures. de Ruggiero was the author of considerable medical research, with the most notable *De Passionibus Mulierum Curandarum* (also known as Trotula Major) which focused on women's health issues. In her *De Ornatu Mulierum* (Trotula Minor) which focused on women's cosmetics), she expounded on how to 'conserve and improve...beauty, and treat skin diseases through a series of precepts [...] and natural remedies' (Cavallo et al 2008, 79). She also provides guidance on how to minimize wrinkles, as well as: 'remove puffiness from face and eyes, remove unwanted hair from the body, lighten the skin, hide blemishes and freckles, wash teeth and take away bad breath, [and prevent] dying hair'; as well as waxing, and treating chapped lips and gums (80). She also provided 'indications to formulate and use ointment and medicative herbs for the face and the hair and she dispensed advices about improving health through vapour baths and massages' (80). She also provided a recipe for an early medieval blusher: 'take root of red and white bryony, clean it, and chop it finely and dry it. Afterward, powder it and mix it with rose water, and with cotton or a very fine linen cloth, we anoint the face and it will induce redness.' (de Ruggiero qtd. in Cavallo et al 2008, 84). Her pragmatic cures 'rarely include prayers, incantations, astrology or other forms of blatant superstition'. Instead, de Ruggiero attributed beauty to a 'healthy body and harmony with the universe' (80); this was in contrast to many other works of the period.

The commercial fabrication of skin care products is also not a recent invention, as there are examples of a Roman cosmetic product unearthed during an excavation in London of a 'Roman temple precinct'. The unguent contained in a 'small tin canister' when tested in a lab for chemical composition was found to contain SnO_2, Tin Oxide. The addition of this to a 'starch/fat base' will in turn confer a 'white opacity' upon application. Therefore, the 'Londinium cream' is believed to 'served as a foundation layer' and aided in the cosmetic purpose of simulating a lighter skin tone (Grew et. al 2013, 35). Laying the foundation (so to speak) for the ubiquitous cosmetic staple to come.

The history of makeup has also gone hand in hand with the publication of treatises about personal appearance. (Something Way Bandy also did, to great success.) In her monograph *Writing Fashion in Early Modern Italy: From Sprezzatura to Satire* (2014). Eugenia Paulicelli describes how the illustrated costume treatises produced during the Italian Renaissance like *Degli Habiti Antichi e Modérni di Diversi Parti di Mondo* published in Venice in 1590 by Cesare Vecellio described (and thereby regulated) societal codes and conduct of personal appearance. He describes 'married and unmarried Neapolitan women [...] as being elegant in their attire and particularly keen on makeup' (110). In his text that accompanies the plates in his publication, Vecellio also provides a description of high-ranking Neapolitan noblewomen:

> They [...] habitually dye their hair blonde with artfully distilled waters, so effective that their hair appears to be silver. They also make up their faces with various powders

and mixtures; it is frequently the case among them that a woman who does not wear make-up is the target of jokes and derision. (Vecellio qtd. in Paulicelli 2014, 110)

The jokes and derision were not only reserved for the women who did not wear makeup, however. There was a particular genre of satire that pilloried the dress, maquillage and conduct of women who *did*. (Then as now, in fact.)

The prevalence of misogynistic satire on the dress of women inspired one Sister Arcangela Tarabotti (1604-1652) to write her own rebuttal. An independent thinker, Tarabottti was forced against her will to become a nun by her family, and then subsequently authored books entitled: *La Tirannia Paterna* (Paternal Tyranny), *L'Inferno Monacale* (The Monastic Hell) among others (Paulicelli 2015, 5). The output of the cloistered nun—who had to surreptitiously smuggle her writings out of the nunnery through noblewomen she did piecework for—is remarkable for both its proto-feminist stance and vocal repudiation of misogyny she found in other contemporaneous writers. In her *Antisatira*, she says: 'Turn somewhat your anger not toward blaming the ornaments of women but toward condemning the modern abuse of male clothing, reduced to far greater vanity than those of women' (64). And she elaborates on this:

There is no shortage of lascivious men, dedicated to hairdos, makeup, smells and perfumes and all those things that are condemned with so much detestation in women by our very kind satirist [Buoninsegni]. (Tarabotti qtd. in Paulicelli, 70)

Touché Sister Aracangela!

Paulicelli notes that the: 'desire of women to look good goes hand in hand with their right to an education and intellectual life, a connection between body and mind...' (178) And observes that this was also the assertion of other Venetian writers who were contemporary to Sister Aracangela: Moderata Fonte and Lucrezia Marinella.

The policing of cosmetics both indirectly and overt, were an ongoing aspect of larger societal censure of women's conduct and appearance. Similar to sumptuary laws, there were many laws governing the appearance enacted to control the agency afforded women to alter their appearance through cosmetics. Oliver Cromwell introduced an 'act against the vice of painting, and wearing black patches, and immodest dresses of women' (Eldridge 2015, 37) during the Tudor era. [For all the good *that* did!] By the 16th C. the glamorous women of Venice, as well as Catherine de Medici, and definitely Elizabeth I all wore makeup that was heavy, leaden— literally, it was made from lead-derived *ceruse*— maquillage.

Use of makeup has also been remarked upon with accompanying associations on the character of the application. These ranged from analysis of formal portraiture: Madame du Pompadour was 'famously portrayed with noticeably rouged cheeks' (Her signature rococo blush pink of course.) As well as literary, Eldridge quotes les frères Goncourt who noted: 'The rouge of the lady of quality was not the rouge of the court, nor the rouge of a courtesan; it was merely a soupçon of rouge, an imperceptible shade' (frères Goncourt qtd. in Eldridge 2015, 39). Even Lola Montez, noted Irish courtesan, and mistress of King Ludwig I of Bavaria published a book on her beauty practices (Eldridge 2015, 74). These visual and written communications at times dictated conduct, in addition to the beauty counsel provided, always communicating the social and cultural mores of the eras in addition to the guiding application of the cosmetics themselves. Then as now, desire for a beautiful face in makeup has always been conjoined to harsh admonishments towards the practices and techniques. The morality politics and policing driving the discourse, is unmistakable.

In the modern context, celebrities from the ballet and the theatre worlds catalyzed the widespread adoption of makeup around the turn of the last century. The twenties 'Flapper' face was heavily made up and accentuated by a dramatic red lip and her dramatic smoky eye, but it was the influence of the nascent cultural form of the cinema that really pushed both the desire for, and ubiquitous adoption of, makeup over the top. This led to the commercialization and establishment of cosmetics as an industry, and eventually our first 'celebrity' makeup artist: Way Bandy!

SONTAG

"We must conquer AIDS before it affects the heterosexual population and the general population.... We have a very strong public interest in stopping AIDS before it spreads outside the risk groups, before it becomes an overwhelming problem". The statement infuriated organizers from AIDS groups who considered AIDS already an "overwhelming problem" and did not consider it a priority of AIDS research to stop the scourge only "before it affects the heterosexual population." Moreover, many gay leaders wondered who had determined that homosexuals were not part of the "general population" that so concerned the Secretary. (581)

Randy Shilts *And the Band Played On: Politics, People, and the AIDS Epidemic* (2011)

The public discourse around AIDS was fundamentally an expression of punitive moralizing, one that named, blamed, and *shamed*. Susan Sontag who had famously chronicled her own battle against cancer, using it as a reflection of the many difficult aspects of Cancer research: public perception, culpability, guilt; turned to AIDS as a subject in her monograph *AIDS and its Metaphors* (1989). Although a conflicted icon of queer culture, vis-à-vis her own closeted sexuality (O'Connell 2020; Mosher 2019), Sontag was nevertheless an indefatigable advocate, vocal supporter of Queer autonomy, and truly loved Gay men. In *Metaphors* Sontag builds on many of the themes that she explored in her previous book about her own illness. However, within this monograph she focusses specifically about AIDS.

Sontag notes that the impacts of AIDS were particularly shattering…devastating for gay men because it came for the face first. She identifies the physical disfigurements that categorize AIDS, and the "dehumanizing" effects this has: "the most terrifying illnesses are those perceived not just as lethal but as dehumanizing, literally so" (38). She contrasts this with a disease like polio, which although also invasive and terrifying, left the face untouched:

Polio's effects could be horrifying - it withered the body - but it did not mark or rot the flesh: it was not repulsive. Further, polio affected the body only, though that may seem ruin enough, not the face. The relatively appropriate, on metaphorical reaction to Polio owes much to the privileged status of the face, so determining of our evaluation of physical beauty and of physical ruin (Sontag 1989, 39).

Also, it must be noted there was a public perception of who was affected by the disease: "polio was construed as typically a disease of children—of the innocent" (56). Men with AIDS did not have that luxury of "innocence" we were seen by the religious Right as sinners and ours was a wrathful retribution of biblical proportions. It concomitantly identified the person afflicted with the worst of societal ignorance and prejudice. AIDS also made young men old practically overnight. Sontag describes the horror of the disease:

AIDS is progressive, a disease of time. Once a certain density of symptoms is attained, the course of the illness can be swift, and brings atrocious suffering. Besides the commonest presenting illnesses (some hitherto unusual, at least in a fatal form, such as a rare skin cancer and a rare form of pneumonia), a plethora of disabling, disfiguring, and humiliating symptoms make the AIDS patient steadily more infirm, helpless, and unable to control or take care of basic functions and needs (Sontag 1989, 21).

She moves into to the realm of analyzing the meaning that was inferred upon the "spoiled identity" of the sufferer:

In recent years some of the onus on cancer has been lifted by the emergence of a disease whose charge of stigmatisation, whose capacity to create spoiled identity, is

143

far greater. It seems that societies need to have one illness which becomes identified with evil, and attaches blame to its "victims", but it is hard to be obsessed with more than one (Sontag 1989, 16).

For generations, the common idea of death had been a death from cancer, and cancer was viewed as a "generic defeat". However, Sontag posits that a society can only have one illness identified with evil, and when the spectre of AIDS appeared as a great ghoulish nightmare in the collective imaginary, Cancer was then relegated to the a less menacing categorization. With AIDs there was a new threat to life, and it very quickly became the novel "rebuke to life and hope" (24). She traces AIDS' metaphoric genealogy, as both an "invasion" (similar to cancer) as well as a "pollution" due to the socio-sexual origins of the virus:

AIDS has a dual metaphoric genealogy. As a micro process, it is described as cancer is: an invasion. When the focus is transmission of the disease, and older metaphor, reminiscent of syphilis is invoked: pollution. One gets it from the blood or sexual fluids of infected people or from contaminated blood products (Sontag 1989, 17).

Plague notions can be easily applied to AIDS, in a way that they could not to cancer or other diseases:

One reason why plague notions were not invoked is that these epidemics did not have enough of the attributes perennially ascribed to plagues. The more important reason is that there has been a shift in the focus of the moralistic exploitation of illness. This shift, to diseases that can be interpreted as judgments on the individual, makes it harder to use epidemic disease as such. for a long time cancer was the illness that best fitted the secular cultures need to blame and punish and censor through the imagery of disease. Cancer was a disease of an individual, and understood as the result not of an action but rather of a failure to act (to be prudent, to exert proper self-control, or to be properly expressive). In the twentieth century it has become almost impossible to moralize about epidemics - except those which are transmitted sexually (Sontag 1989, 56).

The internal versus the external threats. Cancer metastasizes from within. AIDS is an assault from an external source:

> With cancer, the metaphor scans the issue of causality (still a murky topic in cancer research) and picks up at the point at which rogue cells inside the body mutate, eventually moving out from an original site or organ to overrun other organs or systems-a domestic subversion. In the description of AIDS the enemy is what causes the disease, an infectious agent that comes from the outside... (Sontag 1989, 17).

Also, cancer can be treated into full remission and many times cured, With AIDS the viral assault is permanent:

> What makes the viral assault so terrifying is that contamination, and therefore vulnerability, is understood as permanent. Even if someone infected were never to develop any symptoms - that is, the infection remain, or could by medical intervention be rendered, inactive - the viral enemy would be forever within. In fact, so it is believed, it is just a matter of time before something awakens ("triggers") it, before the appearance of the telltale symptoms. Like syphilis known to generations of doctors as the "great masquerader" (Sontag 1989, 20).

As a result of "countless metaphoric flourishes" that had cast cancer as "synonymous with evil" as well as a perceived "betrayal of the body", the result was shame in the patient, a desire to conceal. With AIDS though, the culpability becomes front and centre. This is not a secret internalized invader that randomly arrives in the body, this is a result of an infection, thus "the scandal is not obscure" (24). As Sontag states:

> Most people outside of sub-Saharan Africa who have AIDS know (or think they know) how they got it. It is not a mysterious affliction that seems to strike at random. Indeed, to get AIDS is precisely to be revealed, in the majority of cases so far, as a member of a certain risk group, a community of pariahs (Sontag 1989, 24- 25).

The community of pariahs were overwhelmingly gay men, with all of the inherent judgment, bias (hate) that is the birthright—then and now—of any gay man (or more expansively any openly Queer person):

> Plagues are invariably regarded as judgments on society, and the metaphoric inflation of AIDS into such a judgment also accustoms people to the inevitability of global spread. this is a traditional use of sexually transmitted diseases: to be described as punishment not just of individuals but of a group (general licentiousness) (Sontag 1989, 54).

The supposed "general licentiousness" of the host population was extremely convenient when it came to denying care and research funding to suppress and stem the rising tides of the early years of the AIDS epidemic:

> Making AIDS everyone's problem and therefore a subject on which everyone needs to be educated, charges the anti-liberal AIDS mythologist, subverts our understanding of the difference between "us" and "them"; indeed, exculpates or at least makes irrelevant moral judgments about "them". In such rhetoric the disease continues to be identified almost exclusively with homosexuality, and

specifically the practice of sodomy. "Has America become a country where classroom discussion of the ten Commandments is impermissible, but teacher instructions in safe sodomy are to be mandatory?" Inquires Pat Buchanan, protesting the "foolish" proposal made in the report of the recent presidential commission on the epidemic, chaired by Admiral Watkins, to outlaw discrimination against people with AIDS (Sontag 1989, 65).

And to thereby undermine efforts to bring widespread awareness to the threat and realities as well as recognize it as a larger and very real danger to the general population of contemporary society:

> Not the disease but the appeals heard from the most official quarters "to set aside prejudice and fear in favour of compassion" (the words of the Watkins report) have become a principal target, suggesting as they do a weakening of the society's power (or willingness) to punish and segregate through judgments about sexual behaviour (Sontag 1989, 65).

This all congealed into a ubiquitous dogma of blame and shame: You got it because you deserved it. You are perceived as an abomination against God, and this is your just punishment. There would be no "foolish" efforts made to educate, ameliorate or even extend compassion by the religious right who—then and now—actively influence secular public politics and policy. This hideous (and widespread) rhetoric infected public discourse. Resulting in a blocking of attempts to counter the rising tide of infection and death. Compounding the suffering and terror of those who were living with the new hostile realities of AIDS: *The only good faggot is a dead faggot.*

Soft Versus Hard Deaths

> Our stories have died with us long enough, we mean to
> leave behind some map, some key, for the gay and lesbian
> people who follow—that they may not drown in the lies, in
> the hate that pools and foams like pus on the carcass of
> America. (11)
>
> Paul Monette "Becoming a Man" in *Reflections, The*
> *World of Paul Monette,* 2017.

For anyone that does not know this, AIDS is a really awful, painful and physically degrading way to die. It was not just that so many died young (many older men died too), it was the dying *hard*, and painfully: "etymologically, patient means suffer. It is not suffering as such that is most deeply feared but suffering that degrades" (Sontag 37)". AIDS was *fundamentally* degrading. Sontag contrasts "hard death" from AIDS with the "soft death" from Tuberculosis:

> In contrast to the soft death imputed to tuberculosis, AIDS,
> like cancer, leads to a hard death. The metaphorized
> illnesses that the collective imagination are all hard deaths,
> or envisaged as such. Being deadly is not in itself enough
> to produce terror. It is not even necessary, as in the
> puzzling case of leprosy, perhaps the most stigmatized of
> all diseases, although rarely fatal and extremely difficult to
> transmit (Sontag 1989, 38).

As Randy Shilts so clearly identified, the "social acceptability" of the patient in turn directly affected the social pressure to find a cure:

> Legionnaires disease hit a group of predominantly white,
> heterosexual middle-aged members of the American

148

Legion. The respectability of the victims brought them a degree of attention and funding for research and treatment far greater than that made available so far to victims of Kaposi's Sarcoma. I want to emphasize the contrast because the "more popular" Legionnaires disease affects fewer people (and proved less likely to be fatal). What society judged was not the severity of the disease but the social acceptability of the individuals afflicted with it (Shilts 2011, 117).

The meaning that was applied to the illness was a direct result of the means of transmission:

I want to emphasize the contrast, because the more popular Legionnaire's disease affected fewer people and proved less likely to be fatal. What society judged was not the severity of the disease but the social acceptability of the individuals affected with it.... I intend to fight any effort by anyone at any level to make public health policy regarding Kaposi's sarcoma or any other disease on the basis of his or her personal prejudices regarding other people's sexual preferences or life-styles (Shilts 2011, 117).

Sexual stigmatization, therefore, determined the care offered to those living with HIV [at that time, more often dying from it], or in the case of fullblown AIDS not offered at all at times.

Sontag advocates challenging this "inexorable process whereby diseases acquire meanings (by coming to stand for the deepest fears)" (Sontag 1989, 94). Citing a liberatory potentiality to the detachment of disease from metaphor, and attributed meanings:

The age-old, seemingly inexorable process whereby diseases acquire meanings (by coming to stand for the deepest fears) and inflict stigma is always worth challenging, and it does seem to have more limited credibility in the modern world, among people willing to be modern - the process is under surveillance now. With this illness, one that elicits so much guilt and shame, the effort to detach it from these meanings, these metaphors, seems particularly liberating, even consoling. but the metaphors cannot be distanced just by abstaining from them. They have to be exposed, criticized, belabored, used up (Sontag 1989, 94).

This would indeed have been liberating for men suffering from AIDS. A challenge to the tribal, hive mind, knee-jerk automatic response to plague-like illness: traditionally banishment or execution.

The first men to battle AIDS were weathering simultaneous assaults both from within their own bodies as their immune systems shut down and left them prey to a host of opportunistic infections, as well as the assaults from without as an accusatory bellowed invocation of fire-and-brimstone religious bile rained down upon them. A force of bias and hatred that actively (highly effectively) worked to withhold research, education, funds and needlessly impeded the search for a cure. There was nowhere to hide from this bilious barrage, as the disease publicly marked those that were living with it.

The disease was so disfiguring at times that people didn't want to be seen in public. I remember seeing men in restaurants, at the gym, on the street; they had it and you knew it, it was written all over their faces. My friends developed painful looking rashes on their necks visible above the shirtline, blistered lesions on their faces, backs of their hands and arms, they wasted down to their sinews, it was heartbreaking.

My friends spoke to me out of bodies that disease had taken over, bodies that were rapidly killing them. There is a particular feeling of helplessness and uselessness that comes from trying to be a supportive friend, pretending everything is normal and fine, even as people you love are dying in front of you. The unmitigated terror those men felt as they fought so bravely, even as the public discourse damned and vilified them. It burns me with a bitter gall in the pit of my stomach to this day. Damn *thee* false prophets, I say.

Written *in* the Body

It is easy to dismiss the many (some, frankly strange) alternative healing modalities that Way Bandy practiced. His soaking of vegetables in bleach, the obsession with nutrition and vitamins, the prohibition on food combining, the protractor and the pendulum, the prohibition on *"putrefication"*! (Bandy qtd. in Cunningham 1976, 127). Taken as an aggregate, it all becomes somewhat comical. But it wasn't like science was offering anything more substantial.

There was nothing else.

A healthy body is an incredible dynamo of vitality. Young men are not accustomed to thinking of every stimulus that comes their way as a threat. AIDS mediation was soon all encompassing. Macrobiotics, meditation, crystals have all attained mythical status in their possibilities for self-healing. Louise L. Hay in *The*

AIDS Book: Creating a Positive Approach (1988) advised the affirmation: "I am willing to forgive" (136). Maybe, but given that these poor men were being subjected to a full out assault on person as well as psyche, forgiveness seemed premature.

At the advent of AIDS, there was absolutely nothing that was effective. It was a roulette wheel, you tested positive, then full blown AIDS. Some survived, many quickly died. What choice did these men have but to seek cures, no matter how tenuous, or desperate?

Alternative healing modalities have had remarkable successes over the millennia (Murphy 1992). The power of focused thought, of receiving the energies of spirit have created a multitude of miracles. It has happened too many times for it not to be a truth. To deny otherwise is a choice. It is a mistake though to reduce the frankly miraculous to some formulaic procedure, one that can be achieved unilateral success.

As Andrew Hollern recounts in *Chronicle of a Plague, Revisited, AIDS and its Aftermath* (2008):

> But Cosmo loved life, treasured his body, was only thirty-five, succeeded in his career, and had much to look forward to. He didn't hate himself, sex, or life. His death did not illuminate anything that leaves us morally edified, or superior, or enlightened—it was just part of the vast human waste that is occurring; just mean and nasty (Holleran 2008, 16-17).

People cannot be blamed for either illness or death. A nasty subtext of blame: "you did not want it enough, you were unable to align yourself with the correct healing energy or treatment" was subtext of much of the "New Age" messaging. Truth is, you can't just pop a coin in a cosmic gumball machine and snatch the miracle that drops out. Illness is complex and biological, and miracles all too rare.

Also, a belief in a God that rewards the devout must by definition co-create a selfsame God that punishes the unworthy. Miraculous healing occurs, I have seen it. But far more often, *too often*, people just die.

Good people die.

Sa mort fut fidèle à sa vie.

"Madame de pompadour ne démentit en ces derniers moments. Sa mort fut fidèle à sa vie. La favorite, un soupçon de rouge sur les joues, fut convenable dans ce spectacle suprême comme dans une pièce apprise: et l'on eût dit que l'agonie était sa dernière comédie et son rôle d'adieux." (396)[1]

Les frères Goncourt comment on the death of *Madame de Pompadour* in their eponymous treatise on the grade dame of the Ancien Régime, 1881

When asked who was your most successful makeover? Way Bandy answered: "Myself I guess" (Bandy qtd. in Lavin 1981, 2B). He remade himself

[1] "Madame de Pompadour did not deny it in these last moments. Her death was true to her life. The favourite, a hint of red on the cheeks, was appropriate in this supreme spectacle as in a learned play: and one would have said that the agony was her last comedy and her farewell." Translation: author.

completely and made sure the past stayed firmly in the past. His was not an open book, in spite of the generously expressive and detailed (extremely successful) beauty and self-care publications he authored. When he was alive, he also did not disclose the terrifying truth that he was living with AIDS. The stigma of AIDS was career destroying; especially for makeup artists because they were in such close contact with the models. They definitely did not want people to know their status, or they wouldn't book jobs. Thus, Bandy told no one, instead he was gargling water to which he had added an eyedropper of bleach.

No one knew until he collapsed at Scavullo's Studio: "When he walked in...I knew he was ill. He looked like an El Greco. He was painfully thin. He must have been sick, but nobody noticed. No one knew he was sick. He never showed any signs." (Scavullo qtd. in Trebbe 1986, 15). Scavullo suppressed his initial AIDS panic:

> My first instinct was not to let him in my apartment and then I thought, you bastard...So I took him up and massaged him and gave him tea, and gave him love and support (Scavullo qtd. in Trebbe 1986, 15).

After the physical collapse at Scavullo's studio that morning in August 1986, Bandy's panicked agent called upon Grace Mirabella, then editor-in-chief of Vogue for assistance. Mirabella's M.D. husband persuaded Bandy to check into the New York Hospital-Cornell Medical Centre the very next day. According to Dr. Catherine C. Hart, the primary cause of death was:

> [P]neumocystis carinii pneumonia and that the "predisposing" secondary cause of death was "an associated HTLV-3-related disease." The HTLV-3 virus,

most scientists believe, is the cause of AIDS, or acquired immune deficiency syndrome, the fatal disease that cripples the body's immune system (Hart qtd. in NYT, 1986).

Bandy only lived for two more weeks.

Akin to Hilarion in *Giselle*, dancing with Myrtha and the wilis until he drops dead of exhaustion: "There was nothing downbeat about his life and there will be nothing downbeat about his death," (Murray qtd. in Folkart 1986). At this point friends did rally around the dying man: "I knew when he was in the hospital he wanted me to hold his hand. So I did. And I'm glad I did. My first instinct was to run. Thank God the better half of me came through." (Scavullo qtd. in Trebbe 1986, 15). Bandy did everything to keep up appearances until the very end:

> He did the whole thing very beautifully. He was very strong. Very gallant. I hope that I can face death one-half, one-tenth as well as he did. He was cracking jokes. He didn't want to upset anybody (Scavullo qtd. in Trebbe 1986, 15).

Tragically, for Way Bandy there would be no reprieve, there was no Giselle to keep him alive until dawn. The medications that stabilize and combat AIDS, and thereby prolong life, were still a year away from public distribution (Ryan 2016) on the day he died.

Bandy took his last breath listening to Maria Callas as she sang the third act of Tosca, as it played on a cassette in his hospital room (Polman 1986). It was a Wednesday, August 13, 1986. "Papa Don't Preach" by Madonna (another Bandy client) was a number one hit song. If you were a gamer you were probably playing *Into the Eagle's*

Nest (onthisday.com). *Blue Velvet*, directed by David Lynch, was one of the most viewed movies released that year. The president was Ronald Reagan, Margaret Thatcher was Prime Minister of England, Brian Mulroney was the Prime Minister of Canada. Pope John Paul II was leading the Catholic Church.

Of note, Bandy's adult universe was not the solitary purgatory of his childhood. His life was shared with a loving partner: Michael Gardine; a "writer, antique dealer and chain smoker" whom he met at a nightclub in 1973. If the fastidious vegetarian Bandy was the Felix of this self-described "odd couple", then Gardine was his fast-food loving Oscar (Rowes 1978, pgh. 22). Gardine would be the first of the couple lost to AIDS in 1985. Bandy and his close confidante hairstylist Maury Hopson made a pact that if either died first the other would publicly announce the cause (Fried 1994). Hopson honoured this, and publicly eulogized both the extraordinary life and exact cause of death of his dear friend. Hopson would later scatter the ashes of both Bandy and Gardine together in a pine forest in their beloved Key West, Florida (Folkart 1986). Even death did not them part.

Of note, "Live to Tell" by Madonna was also released in 1986. On January 16 of that year, the United States Center for Disease Control (CDC) reported that more people were diagnosed with AIDS in 1985 than in all earlier years combined. The 1985 figures showed an "89% increase in new AIDS cases compared with 1984. Of all AIDS cases to date, 51% of adults and 59% of children have died". The report stated that on average, "AIDS patients die about 15 months after the disease is diagnosed." Public health experts predicted that there would be twice as many new AIDS cases in 1986 (hiv.gov). Bandy that impenetrable Sphinx in life proved to be entirely the opposite in death, he was one of the first to have his cause of death publicly announced to have been from AIDS. He bravely ensured that his fame and legacy would be used to highlight the fact that so many were now dying of AIDS in the mid 1980's (Trebbe 1986). He knew that the pariah status of his illness would now (and forever) enshroud him, but he chose to have his executor publicly broadcast this information. Bandy did not "live to tell", but he still communicated posthumously (loudly and unequivocally) that his death was from AIDS.

"He always looked so good," Grace Mirabella stated at Way Bandy's memorial (Mirabella qtd. in Polman 1986). Bandy would have *loved* to hear that, no doubt. Physical attractiveness as a correlation of value and worth were core beliefs for him. He spoke about beauty and where he felt it derived from:

> I believe in reincarnation...That we have many lifetimes. One soul reappears in many bodies. People are rewarded for what they did in their former lives by being given gifts like grace and beauty. I think we earn the way we look (Bandy qtd. in Lavin 1981, 2B).

He positions it as a form of cosmic remuneration. A karmic payback for good deeds done in a previous lifetime, a grand reward of some kind.

I agree wholeheartedly, but I question his parameters for inclusion as well as his definitional criteria. I talk (and think) a lot about beauty and aesthetic properties throughout my work. I am very aware that the standards of beauty can be cruel, exclusionary, and punishing. Honestly though, I still really love to experience the many myriad forms of beauty that there are manifest in this world. However, what I perceive to be beautiful is not always based on physical attributes, or a product of creative labour. Certainly not it its entirety, definitely not anymore. Grace is the key word that resonates for me in Bandy's philosophy. The ennoblement of the spirit of rising above adversity to reach a state of dignity. Now *that* is beautiful. To consciously live a beautiful life.

If there is anything to be taken from the life of the gracile Way Bandy, for me it is his style, and his ability to integrate healing modalities and life-affirming principles into both his métier as well as his guiding philosophy. His oeuvre as a whole was a communication of much larger messages of self-care, and mind-body awareness; it went far deeper than the "cosmetic". His health regime was bizarre at times [truly], but it did reflect a genuine awareness of the importance of holistic connectivity.

To conclude this chapter, I now hand it over to Bandy himself and some "Bandy-Aids", *bon mots* on life and beauty that he shared in 1976 with *Cosmopolitan* in "Way Bandy: Beauty's Darling"—an essay (and title!) that I can only define with the Spanish adjective *sabroso* [so tasty]—published at the height of his popularity and fame:

Bandy Aid for the Working Girl
(*Cosmopolitan* 1976)

Fluorescent office lights are *death*. Nothing, but nothing makes you look so ghoulish. Harsh makeup shows up, color fades or becomes unflatteringly purply. Use rose and peach blushers. Never wear purple, mint green, fuchsia, Royal blue. *Do* wear tinted sunglasses: Rose and amber. Even a hat. Block overhead light if you can. Keep lamps lit at an end table height. When people enter, try to face them into direct light (flattering in the morning) or end of the day or against backlighting (*hides everything*) (Bandy qtd. in Cunningham 1976, 129).

Bandy Do's

- Use as light a foundation as possible: dilute makeup with freshener, mineral water. Avoid opaque mask look.

- Crayon white highlight into indentations: eye bags, mouth creases.

- Stick to natural shades: brown, beige, peach.

- Brush eyebrows up. Widens eyes!

- Use an eyelash curler.

- Make up at your desk before or after work to be sure you look well in office light.

- Mix foundation in different shades to match your skin.

- Highlight just under eyebrows.

- Apply lipstick last, not first, and not from a tube. Special tip: take photographs often. Going to a Photomaton Booth to check on how things are going along. [this last statement only feels anachronistic until one checks their mug with their phone…]

Goal: give the impression of color without coverage. A moist, natural face is the prettiest face of all. (Bandy qtd. in Cunningham 1976, 129)

Conclusion: Counting the Eyeglasses

> You start to think of contempt as a virus. affecting individuals first, but spreading rapidly through families, communities, people, power structures, nations. Less flashy than hate. More deadly. When contempt kills you, it doesn't have to be a vendetta or even entirely conscious. It can be a passing wind. It's far more common, and therefore more lethal. "The virus doesn't care about you." And likewise with contempt: in the eyes of contempt, you don't even truly rise to the level of a hated object – that would involve a full recognition of your existence. (73)

Zadie Smith "Postscript: Contempt as a Virus"
Intimations: Six Essays 2020

I visited Auschwitz in the early 90s, with a group of artists when I was participating in an international art symposium in Poland. We were staying in Krakow, a beautiful medieval town that was spared during the Second World War (and also the First). What had once been the Jewish ghetto was indicated by a façade of gravestones bricked up into a wall. There were two old men sitting there near the wall. There was no longer a Jewish quarter in Krakow.

It was a disconcertingly gorgeous late summer afternoon when we visited the concentration camp, people had brought picnics and were eating on the grass outside the gates. We entered under that terrible metalwork sign *Arbeit Macht Frei* "Work Makes You Free".

Among the horrors that we saw there: the ovens, the barracks, the museum which screened the unbelievably disturbing, yet fundamentally valuable films documenting the Holocaust. I had seen the footage before but viewing it *onsite* was unspeakable.

The physical traces that are still extant onsite are equally devastating:

> [M]ore than a ton of human hair; 110,000 shoes; 3,800 suitcases; 470 prostheses and orthopedic braces; more than 88 pounds of eyeglasses [...] as well as hundreds of hairbrushes and toothbrushes (Donadio 2015, pgh. 5).

There are also "246 prayer shawls; [and] more than 12,000 pots and pans carried by Jews who believed that they were simply bound for resettlement" (Donadio 2015, pgh.5). Twelve...thousand...pots and pans.

The entire camp has been left as a memorial, in fact it is maintained and conserved to stand as a physical record of the atrocity. We walked through rooms filled to the roof with only one item: suitcases, clothes, shoes...human hair?! The revolting systematic efficiency of the Third Reich on evidence along with the material records of the deceased.

There was also a room that contained eyeglasses. Thousands and thousands and thousands of eyeglasses. There was a pile that must have been 7 or 8 feet high, covering most of the room. It was from these that there was an extrapolation of others that were lost in the

Holocaust, as only a smaller portion of the population wears glasses, the existence of one pair stands as a placeholder or identifier of the other percentage of the population who didn't wear glasses. There are many that did not leave a physical trace behind of their existence. Counting the eyeglasses enumerated the others who left no traces.

Directed hate is certainly not specific to Queers, and of course we were targeted and exterminated by the Third Reich as well, which has left us with the enduring symbol of the Pink Triangle (O'Connell 2020). A mnemonic whose significance must never be forgotten.

We do not have a record of all those we lost to AIDS. A description of their beautiful lives lived before their untimely end. I therefore count proverbial eyeglasses to connect with those that were not identified. There is no official memorial to those we lost to AIDS, as Sarah Schulman states:

> The names of our friends whom Ronald Reagan murdered are not engraved in a tower of black marble. There has never been a government inquiry into the fifteen years of official neglect that permitted AIDS to become a worldwide disaster (Schulman 2012, 48).

Then she angrily poses the question:

> "[W]here is our permanent Memorial?" (48)

Yes, where?

END BEGINNING

This is definitely *not* the end, the writing of this has spurred on more inspirations that are larger than the scope of a single monograph. The genie is out of the bottle. Therefore, all will be continued in future *Lilac Time at the Rodeo*, books where we will look at such bright lights as the Cockettes; Tim Jocelyn; Patrick Kelly, General Idea; Stephen Varble/Marie Debris, Scottt Barrie; David Wojnarowicz; Peter Hujar; Miguel Piñero; Martin Wong; Willi Smith and so many more!

Acknowledgments

Heartfelt thank you to my two dedicated readers: Alexandra and Anita, who read each chapter upon completion, and provided invaluable feedback. Thank you to my mum dr. Kathleen O'Connell & my family; Celia McBride; Cheryl Thompson; Roddo, Patrick & Barry; Lee Anne McAlear & Jim Harris; John Sabulis; Georgia Kennedy; Valerie Steele & Peter McNeill; The

Sartorial Society Series; The Seneca College Fashion Resource Centre.

References

To conserve paper, and for easier access when reading, references are available online on my website:

https://markoconnellstudio.com/2021/12/19/rodeo-references/

Follow me on socials!
Instagram

@MARKOCONNELLSTUDIO

TikTok: @markoconnell176

markoconnellstudio

Let others follow you by scanning your QR code

♪ TikTok

LinkedIn:

Dr. Mark Joseph O'Connell
Professor at Seneca Polytechnic

Facebook: markoconnellstudio

X: ProfMOConnell

Manufactured by Amazon.ca
Bolton, ON

36841837R00092